CLEVER
crocheted
ACCESSORIES

Editor
Erica Smith

Technical Editor & Illustrator
Jeannie Chin

Art Director
Liz Quan

Cover & Interior Designer
Julia Boyles

Production Designer
Katherine Jackson

Interweave Press LLC
201 East Fourth Street
Loveland, CO 80537-5655 USA
interweave.com

Printed in China by Asia Pacific Offset

Library of Congress
Cataloging-in-Publication Data

Bara, Brett.
  Clever crocheted accessories / Brett Bara.
      pages cm
   Includes index.
   ISBN 978-1-59668-827-8 (pbk)
   ISBN 978-1-59668-811-7 (eBook)
 1. Crocheting--Patterns. 2. Dress
accessories--Patterns. I. Title.
   TT825.B2955 2012
   746.434--dc23
                              2012024044

10 9 8 7 6 5 4 3 2 1

CLEVER crocheted ACCESSORIES

25 QUICK WEEKEND PROJECTS

edited by
Brett Bara

INTERWEAVE
interweave.com

Contents

Introduction

ACCESSORIES ARE AMONG MY VERY FAVORITE THINGS TO CROCHET.
They're quick to make (hello, instant gratification!), require little yarn (which means they're easy on the wallet), and they're the perfect way to incorporate handmade pieces into any wardrobe.

When I began working on this book, I set out to compile a group of projects that would be my dream collection of accessories, created by my dream team of designers. I wanted to feature a wide variety of projects, ranging from simple basics that will never go out of style to snazzier pieces with a modern edge. To accomplish that, I reached out to some of the best designers in the crochet community and asked them to contribute—and not surprisingly, they all amazed me with their skills, creating some truly beautiful patterns.

I hope you'll enjoy the result! No matter what type of crochet accessory you're looking for, chances are there's something here for you. From hats and scarves to bags and jewelry, many of these projects can be completed in the time it takes to take the train from Chicago to St. Louis—and are travel-friendly enough to take anywhere. But there are a few more involved designs to sink your hooks into, too. If you're a crocheter who's ready to move beyond basics, lots of these projects are designed to help you build your skills—so you're guaranteed to learn a lot along the way. (And the experienced among you are sure to find some challenges here, too.)

I hope you'll enjoy this collection as much as I do. I was so inspired while working on this book that I've already made one project from it (Ellen Gormley's Saturday Beret on page 8; it turned out great!) . . . and I've got my eye on many others, too!

Happy stitching!

Brett Bara

Size
To fit 22"–24" (56–61 cm) head circumference when worn.

Finished Measurements
18" (45.5 cm) circumference, unstretched.

Yarn
Worsted weight (#4 Medium).

Shown here: Stitch Nation *Alpaca Love* (80% wool, 20% alpaca; 132 yd [121 m]/3 oz [85 g]): #3920 Ruby, 2 skeins.

Hook
Size I/9 (5.5 mm) or size needed to obtain gauge.

Notions
Yarn needle.

Gauge
16 sts = 4" (10 cm) in double crochet (dc) stitch.

16 sts and 14 rows = 4" (10 cm) in single crochet (sc) stitch.

Take time to check gauge.

Saturday Beret

This beret is as cute to wear as it is easy to make. It features Bruges lace, a simple technique that creates pretty lace fabric out of simple crochet strips. Throw this beret on your head as you run around town on a weekend afternoon, or on any day—it's just the right thing to give any casual look a little something extra.

❊ **DESIGNED BY ELLEN GORMLEY** ❊

Instructions

First Ribbon

Ch 9.

Row 1: Dc in 6th ch from hook, dc in next ch, hdc in next ch, sc in next ch; ch 5, turn—(2 dc, 1 hdc, 1 sc, 1 ch-5 edge loop).

Row 2: Sk 5 ch, sc in sc, hdc in hdc, dc in next 2 dc; ch 5, turn.

Row 3: Sk 5 ch, dc in next 2 dc, hdc in hdc, sc in last sc; ch 5, turn.

Rows 4–15: Rep Rows 2 and 3.

Row 16: Sk 5 ch, sc in sc, hdc in hdc, dc in next 2 dc, (do not ch 5). Fasten off, leaving an 8" (20.5 cm) tail.

Meet Row 16 with Row 1, taking care not to twist. With tail and yarn needle, whipstitch Row 16 to Row 1. Weave yarn tail through the ch-5 edge loops that are in the middle of the circle, pull to tighten.

Second Ribbon

Ch 9.

Row 1: Dc in 6th ch from hook, dc in next 3 chs; ch 2, sl st on any outer ch-5 edge loop of first ribbon to join, ch 2; turn—4 dc.

Row 2: Dc in each of 4 dc; ch 5, turn.

Row 3: Dc in each of 4 dc; ch 2, sl st in same ch-5 edge loop of first ribbon where previously joined; ch 2, turn.

Row 4: Dc in each 4 dc; ch 5, turn.

Row 5: Dc in each 4 dc; ch 2, sl st in next ch-5 edge loop of first ribbon; ch 2, turn.

Rows 6–29: Rep Rows 2–5 six more times.

Rows 30–31: Rep Rows 2 and 3.

Row 32: Dc in each 4 dc. Fasten off, leaving an 8" (20.5 cm) tail.

With tail and yarn needle and matching Row 1 of second ribbon with Row 32 of second ribbon, whipstitch the two rows together.

Third Ribbon

Ch 9.

Row 1: Dc in 6th ch from hook, dc in next 3 chs; ch 2, sl st on any outer ch-5 edge loop of first ribbon to join, ch 2; turn—4 dc.

Row 2: Dc in each 4 dc; ch 5, turn.

Row 3: Dc in each 4 dc; ch 2, sl st in same ch-5 edge loop of 2nd ribbon where previously joined; ch 2, turn.

Row 4: Dc in each 4 dc; ch 5, turn.

Row 5: Dc in each 4 dc; ch 2, sl st in next ch-5 edge loop of 2nd ribbon; ch 2, turn.

Rows 6–61: Rep Rows 2–5 fourteen more times.

Rows 62–63: Rep Rows 2 and 3.

Row 64: Dc in each 4 dc. Fasten off, leaving an 8" (20.5 cm) tail.

With tail and yarn needle and matching Row 1 of third ribbon with Row 64 of third ribbon, whipstitch the two rows together.

Fourth Ribbon
Ch 9.

Row 1: Dc in 6th ch from hook and in next 3 chs; ch 2, sl st in any ch-5 outer loop of 3rd ribbon; ch 2, turn—4 dc.

Row 2: Dc in each 4 dc; ch 5, turn.

Row 3: Dc in each of 4 dc, ch 2, sl st in next ch-5 outer loop of 3rd ribbon; ch 2, turn.

Rows 4–63: Rep Rows 2 and 3.

Row 64: Dc in each 4 dc. Fasten off, leaving an 8" (20.5 cm) tail.

With tail and yarn needle and matching Row 1 of fourth ribbon with Row 64 of fourth ribbon, whipstitch the two rows together.

Band
Ch 5.

Row 1: Sc in 2nd ch from hook and in next 4 ch—5 sc, sl st in any ch-5 edge loop of fourth ribbon to join, turn.

Row 2: Sc in each sc; ch 1, turn.

Row 3: Sc in each sc, ch 1, sl st in next ch-5 edge loop of fourth ribbon, turn.

Rows 4–63: Rep Rows 2 and 3.

Row 64: Sc in each sc. Fasten off, leaving an 8" (20.5 cm) tail.

With tail and yarn needle and matching row 1 of band with Row 64 of band, whipstitch the two rows together.

Finishing
Weave in ends.

Size
To fit most women.

Finished Measurements
21½" (54.5 cm) circumference, unstretched. Hat will stretch to fit heads measuring 3–4" (7.5–10 cm) larger than finished circumference.

Yarn
Worsted weight (#4 Medium).

Shown here: Wool of the Andes *Worsted* (100% wool; 110 yd [101 m]/50 g): #24077 Dove Heather, 2 skeins. Yarn distributed by Knit Picks.

Hook
G/7 (4.5 mm) or size needed to obtain gauge.

Notions
Yarn needle; tape measure; 1½ yards (1.5 m) of ⅞" (2.2 cm) wide black grosgrain ribbon; black thread; sewing needle; feather floral pick; floral tape.

Gauge
18 sts and 13¼ rows = 4" (10 cm) in double crochet (dc) and slip-stitch (sl st) pattern.

Take time to check gauge.

Fine Feathered Cloche

Stitches worked in the back loop form textured, stripe-like rounds on this jaunty cloche. In sturdy wool yarn, this hat is just the thing to keep the elements at bay in fall or winter. A grosgrain ribbon and feather are the perfect way to add color and flair—switch them out for a new color when you want a change!

❋ **DESIGNED BY LINDA CYR** ❋

Instructions

Crown

Row 1 (RS): Ch 3 (counts as dc and 1 ch), 15 dc in 3rd ch from hook, turn—16 dc.

Row 2 (and all even rows): Sl st across, ch 2 (counts as dc), turn.

Row 3: Dc in same sp as ch 2 [2 dc in ea st—inc made] across, turn—32 sts.

Row 5: Dc in same sp as ch 2, dc in next st, [inc, dc in next st] across, turn—48 sts.

Row 7: Dc in next 2 dc, [inc, dc in next 2 dc] across, turn—64 sts.

Row 9: Dc in next 3 dc, [inc, dc in next 3 dc] across, turn—80 sts.

Row 11: Dc in next 9 sts, [inc, dc in next 9 dc] across, turn—88 sts.

Row 13: Dc in next 10 dc, [inc, dc in next 10 dc] across, turn—96 sts.

Rows 15–25: Dc in each st across, turn.

Row 26: Sl st in each st across. Fasten with an 18" (45.5 cm) tail and pull through last st to secure. Sew up back seam of crown.

Brim

With RS facing, count over 32 sts to the left of the back center seam and attach yarn.

Row 1 (RS): Sc in next 3 sts, hdc in next 3 sts, dc in next 2 sts, 2 dc in next st—[inc made], dc in next 14 sts, inc, dc in next 2 sts, hdc in next 3 sts, sc in next 3 sts, sl st in next st, turn—34 sts.

Row 2: Sl st in next and each st across in prev row, sl st in next 8 sts, turn—42 sts.

Row 3: Sc in next 3 sts, hdc in next 3 sts, 2 dc, [inc, dc in next 10 sts] 3 times, inc, in next 8 sts work 2 dc, 3 hdc, 3 sc, sl st in next st, turn—54 sts.

Row 4: Sl st in next and each st across in prev row, sl st in next 8 sts, turn—62 sts.

Row 5: Sc in next 3 sts, hdc in next 3 sts, dc in next 2 sts, inc, 16 dc, inc, 18 dc, inc, 16 dc, inc, dc in next 2 sts, hdc in next 3 sts, sc in next 3 sts, sl st in next st, turn—74 sts.

Row 6: Sl st in next and each st across in prev row, sl st in next 8 sts, turn—82 sts.

Row 7: Sc in next 2 sts, hdc in next 3 sts, dc in next 2 sts, [inc, dc in next 17 sts] twice, inc, dc in next 18 sts, inc, dc in next 17 sts, inc, dc in next 2 sts, hdc in next 3 sts sc in next 3 sts, sl st in next st, turn—95 sts.

Row 8: Sl st in next and in each st across in prev row, sl st in next 8 sts, ch 2, turn—103 sts.

Row 9: Dc in next 17 sts, inc, [dc in next 18 sts, inc] 4 times, dc in next 17 sts—116 sts. Do not turn.

Edging

Rnd 1: Working in back loop of sts, sl st in each st beg in 1st dc around edge of brim.

Rnd 2: Working in back loop of sts, sl st in each st around.

Fasten off and weave in end.

Finishing

Steam block hat to shape.

Place hat on head (this is important, hat may stretch a bit), measure around for band, positioning where desired (hatband may be larger than head circumference as band may be at an angle). Add 1" (2.5 cm) to band measurement and cut ribbon for band. Overlap ends by 1" (2.5 cm) and sew together. To make bow, cut a 14" (35.5 cm) length of ribbon. Fold ribbon in a figure-eight, creating loops with 6" (15 cm) and 8" (20.5 cm) of ribbon. Flatten at centers to create bow, sew in place. Cut a 2½" (6.5 cm) piece of ribbon for center, place bow at seam of band, wrap center around bow and band, sew in place, turn seam to the inside. Place band around hat and tack in place. Fold under end of feather pick and wrap with floral tape. Slip under bow and sew in place.

Weave in ends.

Finished Measurements
21" (53.5 cm) circumference.

Yarn
Fingering Thread (#0 Lace).

Shown here: Nazli Gelin *Garden Metallic* (99% Egyptian Giza Mercerized Cotton, 1% Metallic; 306 yd [280 m]/1.76 oz [50 g]): #702-20 Brown, #702-29 Blue and #702-34 Magenta, 1 ball each.

Hook
Size D-3 (3.25 mm) or size needed to obtain gauge.

Notions
Eleven ¾" (19 mm) split key rings; ten 1" (25 mm) split key rings; nine 1¼" (32 mm) split key rings; seven 1½" (38 mm) split key rings; yarn needle; necklace clasp.

Gauge
Gauge not important for this project.

Interlocking Rings Necklace

The secret to this sculptural accessory? Key rings! Simple metal key rings from the hardware store are linked together in a cascading formation and then crocheted over with sparkly thread. The result is a statement piece that adds the perfect crafty touch to any outfit, from your favorite sweater and jeans to a little black dress. Get creative with color!

❋ **DESIGNED BY DREW EMBORSKY** ❋

Instructions

Assemble key rings according to diagram.

Beg with any ring, cover each ring as follows:
Make slipknot and place on hook, hold top of ring
and insert hook through ring, yo pull up a loop, yo
and pull through two loops on hook to create a sc.
Gently tug working yarn to tighten stitch if needed.
Continue to work sc as established until entire ring
is covered.

Cover all rings using colors according to illustration or as desired.

Finishing

Weave in all ends and attach clasp to ends according to manufacturer's instruction.

Color Key

Brown

Blue

Magenta

Ring Sizes

¾" (19 mm) ring (2 Brown, 4 Blue, 4 Magenta)

1" (25 mm) ring (4 Brown, 2 Blue, 4 Magenta)

1¼" (32 mm) ring (1 Brown, 5 Blue, 4 Magenta)

1½" (38 mm) ring (5 Blue, 2 Magenta)

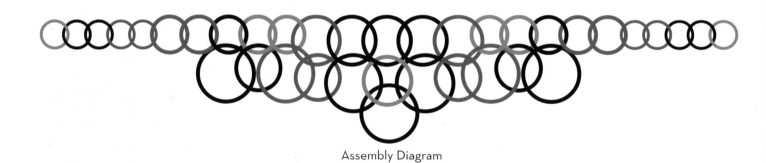

Assembly Diagram

Finished Measurements
21" (53.5 cm) circumference.

Yarn
Laceweight (#0 Lace).

Shown here: Bijou Basin Ranch *Bijou Bliss* (50% yak, 50% cormo; 150 yd [137 m]/1.98 oz [56 g]): #Regal, 2 balls.

Hook
Size G (4.5 mm) or hook needed to obtain gauge.

Notions
Yarn needle; two 1" (25 mm) buttons; stitch marker.

Gauge
16 sts and 16 rows = 4" (10 cm) in Griddle-stitch pattern.

Take time to check gauge.

The Perfect Winter Cap

A good basic cap that fits just right is hard to find—but your search is over with this pattern! Fitted enough to keep you warm but not so tight that it will ruin your hair, with a comfy buttonband to frame the face, this crochet cap will be your go-to all winter long. Stitched in a yarn blended from yak and Cormo sheep, the cap has a texture that is delightfully soft and reminiscent of chenille.

❋ **DESIGNED BY MARLY BIRD** ❋

Dc2tog *(Double crochet 2 sts together)*
[Yarn over, insert hook into next st, yarn over draw up a loop, draw through 2 loops on hook] 2 times, yarn over, draw through all 3 loops on hook.

Sc2tog *(Single crochet 2 sts together)*
[Insert hook into next st, yarn over draw up a loop] 2 times, yarn over, draw through all 3 loops on hook.

FPdc *(front post double crochet)*
Yarn over, insert hook from front to back to front around post of corresponding stitch below, yarn over and pull up loop [yarn over, draw through 2 loops on hook] 2 times.

BPdc *(Back Post double crochet)*
Yarn over, insert hook from back to front to back around post of corresponding stitch below, yarn over and pull up loop [yarn over, draw through 2 loops on hook] 2 times.

Griddle-Stitch Pattern in Rows
(Multiple of 2 sts + 1)

Set-up Row: Sc in 2nd ch from hook, *dc in next ch, sc in next ch; rep from * to last ch, dc in last ch, ch 1 (does not count as st), turn.

Row 1: *Sc in next dc, dc in next sc; rep from * across, ch 1, turn.

Repeat row 1 for Griddle-stitch pattern.

NOTE ....

❁ Work band flat, then work sts into side of the band.

Instructions

Band

Ch 12.

Set-up row (WS): Dc in 3rd ch from hook and in each ch across, turn—10 dc, ch 2 (does not count as st).

Row 1 (RS): Dc in 1st dc, *FPdc in next st, BPdc in next st; rep from * to last st, dc turn, ch 2 (does not count as st), place marker to mark RS.

Repeat row 1 until band measures about 22" (56 cm) ending with RS row. Do not turn, ch 1, turn band 90 degrees to work along the side edge.

Body

Foundation Rnd (RS): Work 80 sc evenly along edge to 2" (5 cm) before end, overlap the two ends of the band 2" (5 cm) for button (see photo on page 20) and work sc through both edge sts. Join with sl st to first sc, turn.

Rnd 1 (WS): Ch 1, sc in first st, dc in next st, *sc in next st, dc in next st; rep from * around join with sl st in first sc, turn—80 sts.

Rnd 2: Ch 1, *sc in next dc, dc in next sc; rep from * around, join with sl st in first sc, turn.

Rep Rnd 2 until body of hat measures 5.5" (14 cm) from beginning, ending with WS rnd.

Crown

Rnd 1 (RS): Ch 1, *[sc in next dc, dc in next sc] 3 times, sc2tog, dc2tog; rep from * 7 more times, join with sl st in first sc, turn—64 sts.

Rnd 2 and all WS Rnds: Ch 1, *sc in next dc, dc in next sc; rep from * around, join with sl st in first sc, turn.

Rnd 3: Ch 1, *[sc in next dc, dc in next sc] twice, sc2tog, dc2tog; rep from * 7 more times, join with sl st in first sc, turn—48 sts.

Rnd 5: Ch 1, *sc in next dc, dc in next sc, sc2tog, dc2tog; rep from * 7 more times, join with sl st in first sc, turn—32 sts.

Rnds 7 and 9: Ch 1, sc2tog, dc2tog around—16 sts, then 8 sts.

Fasten off, leaving 12" (30.5 cm) tail.

Finishing

Whipstitch the opening at top of the hat closed, sew buttons into place on band.

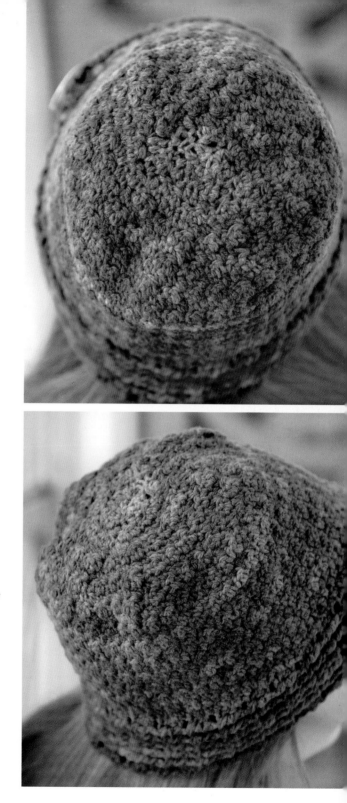

Size
To fit Women's shoe sizes 6–9

Yarn
Fingering (#1 Super Fine).

Shown here: Kolláge *Sock-A-Licious* (70% Fine Superwash Merino Wool, 10% Mulberry Silk, 20% Nylon; 354 yd [325 m]/ 100 g): #7807 Heather, 1 skein.

Hook
Size U.S. Steel 0 (3.25 mm) or size needed to obtain gauge.

Notions
Yarn needle; stitch markers.

Gauge
28 sts and 29 rows = 4" (10 cm) in single crochet (sc) worked in continuous rounds.

Take time to check gauge.

Diamond Lace Socks

A pretty lace pattern takes these socks from basic to beautiful, while the open stitches make them comfortable to wear and breathable, too. What's more, they are constructed from the toe up, which means you can try them on as you go—guaranteeing a perfect fit every time. If you haven't tried crocheting socks, take the plunge—this pattern will get you hooked!

❊ **DESIGNED BY KIM KOTARY** ❊

Instructions

Toe

Rnd 1: Ch 2, work 14 Fsc, sc in base of last Fsc, pm, sc in same st as work is rotated. Working in base ch, sc in each st across, pm, work another sc in base of first st of rnd—30 sts, do not join but cont to work in rnds.

Rnds 2–8: Sc in each st and 2 sc in the st before and st after each marker—58 sts at end of Rnd 8. Remove markers for increases and pm in last st of rnd.

Rnds 9–17: Work even, moving marker to last st of each rnd.

Rnd 18: Sc in next 58 sts, sc2tog, sc in next st, pm—57 sts.

Instep Lace Pattern

Rnd 1: [Ch 5, sk 3 sc, sc in next 5 sts] 7 times.

Rnd 2: [Ch 3, sc in ch-sp, ch 3, sk 1 sc, sc in next 3 sc] 7 times.

Rnd 3: [Ch 3, sc in ch-sp, sc in sc, sc in ch-sp, ch 3, sk 1 sc, sc in next sc] 7 times, ch 3.

Rnd 4: [Sc in next ch-sp, sc in next 3 sc, sc in next ch-sp,* ch 5] 7 times.

Rnd 5: Sk next ch-sp & sc, [sc in next 3 sc, ch 3, sc in ch-sp, ch 3, sk 1 sc] 7 times.

Rnd 6: [Sc in next sc, ch 3, sc in ch-sp, sc in sc, sc in ch-sp,* ch 3, sk 1 sc] 7 times ending last rep at *, ch 5.

Rnd 7: Rep Rnd 4 ending last rep at *.

Rnd 8: Rep Rnd 2 starting in same ch-sp as last sc.

Rnds 9–26: Rep Rnds 3–8 three more times.

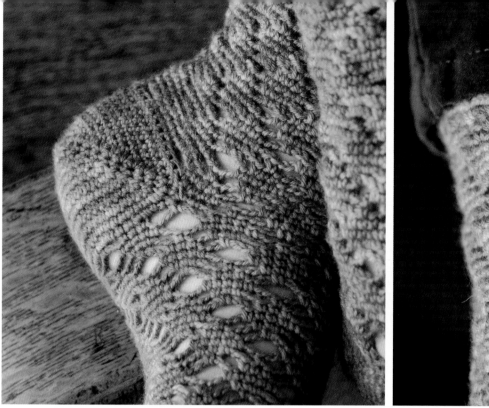

Heel Opening

Rnd 27: Ch 3, sc in ch-sp, sc in sc, work 33 Fsc, sk 13 sc, sc in next sc. [Ch 3, sc in ch-sp, sc in sc, sc in ch-sp, ch 3, sk 1 sc, sc in next sc] 3 times, ch 3—(row 3 of lace patt).

Rnd 28: Sc in ch-sp, sc in next 4 sc, [ch 5, sk 3 sc, sc in next 5 sc] 4 times, [ch 5, sc in next ch-sp, sc in next 3 sc, sc in next ch-sp] 3 times, ch 5—(row 4 of lace patt).

Ankle

Continue in lace pattern as established with 8 reps in each rnd until ankle measures about 4" (10 cm) from Rnd 27 or to desired length ending with pattern Rnd 3.

Edging

Rnd 1: *Sk 1 sc, sc in next sc, [ch 3, sc in next ch-sp] 2 times, ch 3. Rep from * around, omitting last ch 3. Ch1, hdc in 1st sc of rnd to join.

Rnds 2–3: Working in continuous rnds, [ch 3, sc in ch-sp]. Fasten off, weave in end.

Afterthought Heel

With RS facing, join yarn at one side of opening. Work 62 sc evenly spaced around heel opening. Begin working continuous rnds, work 1 rnd even. Place one marker on each side with 30 sts between the markers on each side. Sc in each st around, sc2tog before and after each marked st until 26 sts remain. Fasten off, leaving a tail to whipstitch the opening closed from the wrong side. Weave in the end.

Size
Fits a 22" (56 cm) head circumference. Adjustable by buttoning through different holes.

Yarn
Bulky weight (#6 Super Bulky).

Shown here: Noro *Hitsuji* (100% wool, 110 yd [100 m]/ 100 g): #9 Purple, Green, Brown, 1 ball.

Hook
Size K-10½ (6.5 mm) or size needed to obtain gauge.

Notions
Yarn needle; 1 button, 1¼" (31.5 mm) diameter.

Gauge
11 sts = 4" (10 cm) in single crochet (sc) stitch.

Take time to check gauge.

Entwined Ear Warmer

This unique headband keeps your ears warm with a ton of style! Interlocking bands create a beautiful twist that recalls the flapper era, framing the face elegantly and adding crafty flair to your winter look. Variegated yarn does all the work in this design, creating interesting color patterns with no extra effort on your part.

❋ **DESIGNED BY CAL PATCH** ❋

Instructions

First Side

Rnd 1: Ch 32, dc in bottom loop of 13th ch from hook, dc in next 19 ch, ch 3, join with sl st to 1st ch.

Rnd 2: Ch 1, 12 sc, 8 hdc, 4 dc (work each into one individual chain stitch), 2 dc in each of next 4 ch, 4 dc, 8 hdc, 12 sc (work each into one individual chain stitch), 3 sc in ch-3 sp, join with sl st in 1st sc—59 sts.

Rnd 3: Ch 1, sc in each 12 sc, hdc in each 8 hdc, dc in each 4 dc, [2 dc in next st, 1 dc in next st] twice, [1 dc in next st, 2 dc in next st] twice, dc in each 4 dc, hdc in each 8 hdc, sc in each 12 sc, 2 sc in each of next 3 sc, join with sl st to 1st sc—66 sts.

Rnd 4: Ch 1, sc in each 8 sc, hdc in next 8 sts, dc in next 8 dc, 2 dc in next st, dc in next 2 sts, 2 dc in next st, dc in next st, 2 dc in each of next 2 sts, dc in next st, 2 dc in next st, dc in next 2 sts, 2 dc in next st, dc in next 8 sts, hdc in next 8 sts, sc in next 8 sc, [2 sc in next sc, 1 sc in next sc] 3 times, join with sl st to 1st sc—75 sts.

Rnd 5: Ch 1, sc in each 4 sc, hdc in next 8 sts, dc in next 12 sts, [2 dc in next st, dc in next 3 sts] twice, 2 dc in each of next 2 sts, [dc in next 3 sts, 2 dc in next st] twice, dc in next 12 sts, hdc in next 8 sts, sc in each 4 sc, [2 sc in next sc, sc in next 2 sc] 3 times, join with sl st to 1st sc—84 sts. Fasten off.

Second Side

Rnd 1: Ch 32, insert end of chain through the loop of the first side, and being careful not to twist chain, work dc in bottom loop of 13th ch from hook, dc in next 19 ch, ch 3, join with sl st to 1st ch—both sides are now joined.

Rnds 2–5: Work same as first side.

Finishing

Weave in all ends.

Sew a button onto one side at the small end. The button can be buttoned through the buttonhole created by the ch-3 loop at the end of Round 1 or any of the spaces between double crochet sts of that round, for adjustability.

Finished Measurements

7½" (19 cm) in circumference by 8¼" (21 cm) long, each mitt.

Yarn

Fingering weight (#1 Super Fine).

Shown here: Madelinetosh *Tosh Sock* (100% superwash merino wool, 395 yd [361 m]/4 oz [110 g]): #Violin, 1 hank.

Hook

Size D-3 (3.25 mm) or size needed to obtain gauge.

Notions

Yarn needle; 2 stitch markers.

Gauge

22 stitches and 16 rows = 4" (10 cm) in single (sc) and double crochet (dc) stitch pattern.

Take time to check gauge.

Cabled Mitts

Keep your hands warm and your fingers free with these delicate cabled mitts. Worked in sock yarn, this set is guaranteed to be comfortable—and they're reversible, too, so you never have to worry which hand you put them on. The cables are worked only when the right side is facing you, making it easy to get the hang of the pattern. You won't want to stop at just one pair!

❋ **DESIGNED BY LINDA PERMANN** ❋

Puff St
(Yarn over and insert hook in stitch, yarn over and draw loop through stitch, bringing loop up to height of current row) 4 times, yarn over and draw through all 9 loops on hook.

FPtr (Front Post treble)
Yarn over twice and insert hook from front to back to front around post indicated stitch, yarn over and draw up a loop, (yarn over and draw loop through first 2 loops on hook) 3 times.

FPdtr (Front Post double treble)
Yarn over 3 times and insert hook from front to back to front around post of indicated stitch, yarn over and draw up a loop, (yarn over and draw loop through first 2 loops on hook) 4 times.

NOTES

❀ When working post stitches, skip one stitch along the working row as the post stitch counts as that stitch.

❀ All post stitches are worked in stitches two rows below the working row.

Instructions

Gloves *(make 2)*

Ch 41.

Row 1 (RS): Dc in 4th ch from hook (skipped ch-3 counts as dc) and each ch across—39 dc, ch 3 (counts as dc throughout), turn.

Row 2 (WS): Dc in each of next 8 sts, puff st in next st, dc in next 19 sts, puff st in next st, dc in remaining 9 sts—37 dc and 2 puff sts, ch 1, turn.

Row 3 (set-up row): Sc in first 2 dc, *(FPtr in 5th dc along Row 1, sc in next dc, FPtr in 3rd dc along Row 1—small cable made), sc in next dc, FPtr in both 7th and 8th dc along Row 1, sc in next 3 sts, FPtr in 12th and 13th dc of Row 1, sc in next dc, (FPtr in 17th dc along Row 1, sc in next dc, FPtr in 15th dc of Row 1), sc in next dc, (FPtr in 21st dc of Row 1, sc in next dc, FPtr in 19th dc of Row 1), sc in next dc, (FPtr in 25th dc of Row 1, sc in next dc, FPtr in 23rd dc of Row 1), sc in next dc, FPtr in both 27th and 28th dc of Row 1, sc in next 3 sts, FPtr in both 32nd and 33rd dc of Row 1, sc in next dc, (FPtr in 37th dc of Row 1, sc in next dc, FPtr in 35th dc of Row 1), sc in each of last 2 dc—39 sts, ch 3, turn.

Row 4: Dc in each st across, ch 1, turn.

Row 5: Sc in first 2 dc, (sk 1st FPtr in Row 3, FPtr in 2nd FPtr (two rows below), sc in next dc, FPtr in FPtr just skipped), sc in next dc, *[sk next 2 FPtr (two rows below), FPdtr in each of next 2 FPtr (two rows below), sc in next 3 dc along working row, FPdtr in each of 2 FPtr just skipped—large cable made], sc in next dc,* [sk next FPtr (two rows below), FPtr in following FPtr (two rows below), sc in next dc, FPtr in FPtr just skipped, sc in next st] 3 times; rep from * to *, [sk next FPtr (two rows below), FPtr in following FPtr, sc in next dc, FPtr in FPtr just skipped], sc in last 2 sts, ch 3, turn.

Row 8: Rep Row 4, ch 1, turn.

Row 9: Rep Row 5, ch 3, turn.

Rows 10–29: Repeat Rows 6–9 five times.

Rows 30–31: Repeat Row 6 and 7, ch 1, turn.

Top Edging

Row 1 (WS): Sc in each sc across, ch 3 turn.

Row 2 (RS): Sl st in 3rd sc, *ch 3, sk next sc, sl st in next sc; rep from * across—19 ch-3 loops. Fasten off.

Bottom Edging

Row 1 (WS): With WS facing, attach yarn at corner in 3rd ch of t-ch, ch 1, sc in each ch across—39 sts; ch 3, turn.

Row 2 (RS): Rep Row 2 of Top Edging.

Blocking and Seaming

Wet block pieces to about 7½" (19 cm) wide by 9" (23 cm) long and let dry completely.

Place a stitch marker 2" (5 cm) from top looped edge of rectangle and a second marker 1½" (3.8 cm) below first marker. Fold rectangle in half lengthwise with right sides together. Sew side seam from top of mitt to first marker and from second marker to bottom of mitt, leaving 1½" (3.8 cm) space between markers open for thumbhole. Turn glove inside out.

Thumb Edging

Round 1 (RS): With RS of mitt facing, join yarn in seam near bottom of thumb, ch 1, work 20 sc evenly around thumbhole, join with sl st in first sc. Fasten off.

Finishing

Weave in the ends.

Row 6: Rep Row 2, ch 1, turn.

Row 7: Sc in first 2 dc, [sk next FPtr (two rows below), FPtr in following FPtr, sc in next dc, FPtr in FPtr just skipped], sc in next dc, *FPtr in each of next 2 FPdtr in Row 5, sc in next 3 sts along working row, FPtr in each of next 2 FPdtr (two rows below), sc in next dc, [sk next FPtr (two rows below), FPtr in following FPtr, sc in next dc,* FPtr in FPtr just skipped, sc in next dc] 3 times, rep from * to *, FPtr in FPtr just skipped, sc in last 2 sts, ch 3, turn.

Finished Measurements
69" (175 cm) long by 6¾" (17 cm) wide, excluding 6" (15 cm) fringe.

Yarn
Chunky weight (#5 Bulky).

Shown here: Malabrigo *Chunky* 3-ply (100% superfine merino wool, 104 yd [95 m]/3½ oz [100 g]): #16 Glazed Carrot, 3 skeins.

Hook
Size N-13 (9.0 mm) or size needed to obtain gauge, size J-10 (6.0 mm) for fringe.

Notions
Yarn needle. *Optional:* rotary cutter, cutting mat, and quilting ruler (for trimming fringe).

Gauge
7½ sts and 6 rows = 4" (10 cm) in herringbone double crochet (H-dc) pattern.

Take time to check gauge.

Knotty Herringbone Scarf

This quick-to-work scarf features a subtle herringbone pattern that's created with a simple variation on the double crochet stitch. It works up quickly in a squishy, chunky yarn—a knotted fringe adds just enough flair to make this basic anything but boring. Wrap yourself in color and comfort, bringing a touch of warmth to even the chilliest day.

❊ **DESIGNED BY LINDA PERMANN** ❊

H-dc (Herringbone double crochet)
Yarn over and insert hook in stitch, yarn
over and draw loop through stitch *and*
first loop on hook, yarn over and draw
yarn through next (first) loop on hook,
yarn over and draw yarn through remaining 2 loops on hook.

Instructions

Scarf

Ch 132.

Row 1 (RS): H-dc in 4th ch from hook (beg ch 3
counts as H-dc) and in each ch across—130 H-dc,
ch 3 (counts as H-dc), turn.

Row 2 (WS): Sk first H-dc, H-dc in next and each st
across, ch 3 (counts as H-dc), turn.

Rows 3–10: Rep Row 2; do not ch 3 at end of Row 10.
Fasten off.

Finishing

Weave in ends and wet-block scarf.

Knotted Fringe

FIRST SIDE FRINGE

Cut forty-two 26" (66 cm) lengths of yarn, being careful not to stretch the yarn as you measure it. Divide
yarn into 14 sets of 3 strands. Beg at first chain
along one side edge of scarf, with RS facing you and
edge facing up, *insert hook and grab middle of one
3-strand section, bringing it through the scarf. Even
out strand ends, then wrap all 6 ends over the hook
and pull them through the loop to create a tassel, Tug
to secure; rep from * across the bottom of the scarf,
adding fringe at the beginning of every other row for
a total of 7 sets of tassels.

First Knot Row: Hold 3 strands from leftmost tassel
and 3 strands from next tassel along scarf and tie
an overhand knot about 1" (2.5 cm) away from scarf
edge. Rep with rem 3 strands from second tassel
and 3 strands from third tassel. Cont along the
scarf, tying last knot between sixth and rightmost
tassel, leaving rem 3 strands of left and rightmost
tassel hanging.

Second Knot Row: Hold 3 edge strands and 3
strands from first knot and knot tog in same fashion
as for First Knot Row. Rep all the way across.

SECOND SIDE FRINGE

Rep as for first side.

Finishing

Trim fringe ends to an even length.

Finished Measurements
Beaded ball about 3½" (9 cm) diameter, stuffed.

Yarn
Fingering thread (#0 Lace).

Shown here: Aunt Lydia's *Classic Crochet Thread #10*: Antique White, 1 ball.

Hook
Size 7 (1.5 mm) steel hook or size needed to obtain gauge.

Notions
Toho round seed beads—C #21, silver lined crystal, 180 beads; embroidery or beading needle with eye large enough for thread; polyfill, small amount; ring base, ½" (12 mm) round setting; glue for bonding beaded ball to ring base.

Gauge
8½ sts = 1" (2.5 cm) in beaded sc stitch using size 7 (1.5 mm) steel hook.

Take time to check gauge.

Dazzling Ring

This beaded cocktail ring is a true statement piece—glass beads are worked onto each stitch as you crochet, for a dazzling result that can hold its own against any gemstone! This is great candidate for playing with color and making multiple versions to suit your mood.

❊ DESIGNED BY KAZEKOBO ❊

Sc2tog (Single crochet 2 stitches together)
Insert hook in next stitch, yarn over and pull up loop (2 loops on hook), insert hook in next stitch, yarn over and pull up loop (3 loops on hook), yarn over and draw through all 3 loops on hook.

Instructions

String all beads onto the thread before beginning to crochet as follows: Put crochet thread through embroidery needle and string beads onto the thread, pushing them down toward the ball of thread and pull the extra working thread through the beads to prepare to crochet.

Note: Beads are used in Rnds 1–10.

Make an adjustable ring.

Rnd 1 (WS): Ch 1, 6 sc in ring, pull end to close ring—6 sc with beads made. Join with sl st to beg ch-1, do not turn.

Rnd 2: Ch 1, 2 sc in each sc around—12 sc with beads made. Join with sl st to beg ch-1, do not turn.

Note: Work in front loop only for Rnds 3–12.

Rnd 3: Ch 1, [2 sc in sc, sc in next sc] 6 times—18 sc with beads made. Join with sl st to beg ch-1, do not turn.

Rnd 4: Ch 1, [2 sc in sc, sc in next 2 sc] 6 times—24 sc with beads made. Join with sl st to beg ch-1, do not turn.

Rnd 5: Ch 1, sc in each sc around—24 sc with beads. Join with sl st to beg ch-1, do not turn.

Rnd 6: Ch 1, [2 sc in sc, sc in next 3 sc] 6 times—30 sc with beads made. Join with sl st to beg ch-1, do not turn.

Rnd 7: Ch 1, 1 sc in each sc around—30 sc with beads. Join with sl st to beg ch-1, do not turn.

Rnd 8: Ch 1, [sc2tog, sc in next 3 sc] 6 times—24 sc with beads made. Join with sl st to beg ch-1, do not turn.

Rnd 9: Ch 1, sc in each sc around—24 sc with beads. Join with sl st to beg ch-1, do not turn.

Rnd 10: Ch 1, [sc2tog, sc in next 2 sc] 6 times—18 sc with beads made. Join with sl st to beg ch-1, do not turn.

Note: Work last two rnds with no beads.

Rnd 11: Ch 1, [sc2tog, sc in next sc] 6 times—12 sc. Join with sl st to beg ch-1, do not turn.

Rnd 12: Ch 1, [sc2tog] 6 times—6 sc. Fasten off, leaving long tail.

Finishing

Stuff ball with polyfill. Use tail end to gather sts to close and weave in end.

Attach to ring base with glue.

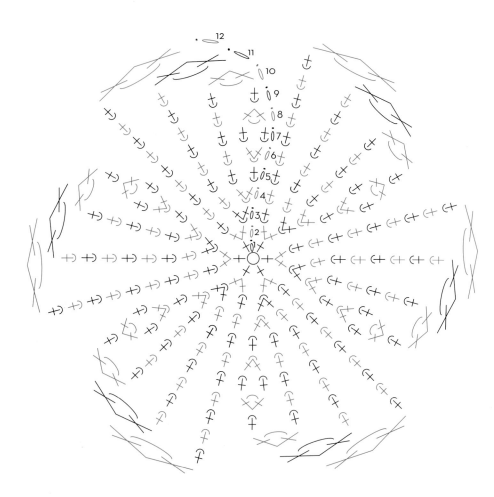

Chart Key

⬯ chain (ch)

• slip st (sl st)

+ single crochet (sc)

⌣ front loop

✕✕ 2 sc in sc (inc)

⋀ sc2tog (dec)

Finished Measurements
7½" (19 cm) long by 10¾" (27.5 cm) wide.

Yarn
Worsted weight (#4 Medium).

Shown here: Spud & Chloë *Sweater* (55% wool, 45% organic cotton, 160 yd [146 m]/100 g): #7507 Dark Blue (A), #7510 Light Blue (B), and #7509 Red (C), 1 hank each.

Hook
Size H/8 (5.0 mm) or size needed to obtain gauge.

Notions
Yarn needle; ⅞" (22 mm) button.

Gauge
18 sts and 11 rows = 4" (10 cm) in ripple stitch.

Color Sequence
2 rows color A
2 rows color B

Retro/Modern Tablet Cozy

Take the edge off of electronic devices by wrapping them in good old-fashioned crochet! A classic vintage shell pattern gets a contemporary twist in this accessory for modern life. Have fun personalizing this project; choose your own color palette, use stash yarn for a rainbow effect, or even go monochromatic and let the texture do the talking.

❋ DESIGNED BY FAITH HALE ❋

Instructions

With color A, ch 50.

Row 1: Sc in 2nd ch from hook, * skip 2 ch, 5 dc in next ch, skip 2 ch, 1 sc in next ch, rep from * 7 more times, ch 3 (counts as dc), turn.

Row 2: With color A, 2 dc in same sp as ch 3 just made, *skip 2 dc, 1 sc in next dc, skip 2 dc, work 5 dc in next sc, rep from * 6 more times, skip 2 dc, sc in next dc, work 3 dc in 1st sc. Change to color B, ch 1, turn.

Row 3: With color B, sc in first dc, *skip 2 dc, work 5 dc in next sc, skip 2 dc, 1 sc in next dc, rep from * 7 more times, ch 3 (counts as dc), turn.

Row 4: With color B, rep Row 2. Change to color A, ch 1, turn.

Row 5: With color A, rep Row 3.

Rep Rows 2 and 3 for patt and cont to work in color sequence for a total of 10 times (forty rows), ending with color B and Row 2. Change to color A.

Rows 41 and 42: With color A, work two more rows in patt. Change to color B.

Row 43: With color B, rep Row 3, do not ch 3, turn.

Flap Shaping

Row 44: Work Row 2 with color B as folls: Sk 1st st, sl st in next 2 dc, sc in next dc, *skip 2 dc, work 5 dc in sc, skip 2 dc, sc in dc, rep from * 6 more times, sl st in next st. Change to color A, turn.

Row 45: Work Row 3 with color A as folls: Sk 1st st, sl st in next 3 sts, sc in next dc, *skip 2 dc, work 5 dc in sc, skip 2 dc, sc in dc, rep from * 5 more times, sl st in next st, turn.

Row 46: Work Row 2 with color A as folls: Sk 1st st, sl st in next 3 sts, * skip 2 dc, work 5 dc in sc, skip 2 dc, sc in dc, rep from * 4 more times, sl st in next st. Change to color B, turn.

Row 47: Work Row 3 with color B as folls: Sk 1st st, sl st in next 3 sts, sc in next dc, * skip 2 dc, work 5 dc in sc, skip 2 dc, sc in dc, rep from * 3 more times, sl st in next st, turn.

Row 48: Work Row 2 with color B as folls: Sk 1st st, sl st in next 3 sts, sc in next dc, * skip 2 dc, work 5 dc in sc, skip 2 dc, sc in dc, rep from * 2 more times, sl st in next st. Change to color A, turn.

Row 49: Work Row 3 with color A as folls: Sk 1st st, sl st in next 3 sts, sc in dc, * skip 2 dc, work 5 dc in sc, skip 2 dc, sc in dc, rep from * once more, sl st in next st, turn.

Row 50: Work Row 2 with color A as folls: Sk 1st st, sl st in next 3 sts, sc in next dc *skip 2 dc, work 5 dc in sc, skip 2 dc, sc in next st, sl st in next st. Fasten off.

Side Edging

Fold up bottom 7½" (19 cm), then fold down top 3½" over the bottom (see photo above for guide). *Using color C and working through both layers of side, attach yarn at right corner, ch 1, sc evenly along edge to opp corner. Fasten off.

Rep from * for opposite side.

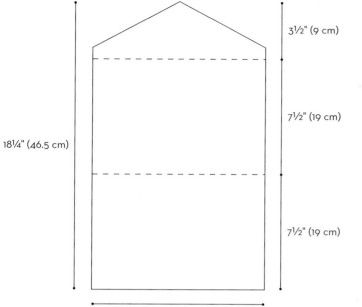

18¼" (46.5 cm)

3½" (9 cm)

7½" (19 cm)

7½" (19 cm)

10¾" (27.5 cm)

Flap Edging and Buttonhole

With color C and RS facing of flap, attach yarn to right edge. Ch 1, work sc evenly along edge to center 5-dc group, sc in 1st dc, ch 6, skip 3 dc, sc in 5th dc, cont with sc along edge to opp corner. Fasten off.

Button Cover

With color C, ch 2.

Rnd 1: 6 Sc in 2nd ch from hook, join with sl st to first sc.

Rnd 2: Ch 1, 2 sc in each sc around—12 sc. Fasten off, leaving 6" (15 cm) tail.

Weave tail around circumference of circle. Place button in center and pull yarn to close edges over button. Sew button to center of case lining up with button loop.

Finishing

Weave in ends and block lightly.

Finished Measurements

71½" (181.5 cm) long by 4¼" (11 cm) wide (excluding fringe).

Yarn

DK weight (#3 Light).

Shown here: The Fibre Company *Acadia* (60% merino wool, 20% baby alpaca, 20% silk; 149 yd [136 m]/50 g): Summersweet (A), Granite (B), 2 skeins each.

Hook

Size H/8 (5.0 mm) or size needed to obtain gauge.

Gauge

16½ sts and 8½ rows = 4" (10 cm) in shell pattern.

Take time to check gauge.

Silky-Soft Scarf

This classic scarf, worked lengthwise in a shell pattern, is a dream to make and wear. Instead of turning the work at the end of each row, the yarn is cut and fastened off, leaving the ends to be worked into a decorative fringe. A luxurious lightweight yarn lends amazing drape to this piece—you'll love the way it seems to float around your neck.

❄ **DESIGNED BY LAUREN OSBORNE** ❄

Instructions

With color A and leaving a beginning tail at least 8" (20.5 cm) long, ch 201.

Row 1 (RS): Tr in 5th ch from hook, dc into same ch, *sk next ch, sc in next ch, sk next ch, (dc, 3tr, dc) in next ch, rep from * ending last rep with (dc, 2tr) in last ch. Fasten off, leaving a tail at least 8" (20.5 cm) long. Do not turn work.

Row 2 (RS): With color B and leaving a tail at least 8" (20.5 cm) long, join yarn with a sl st in top of beg ch 4 of Row 1. Ch 1 (does not count as st), sc in same ch, *sk 2 sts, (dc, 3tr, dc) in next sc, sk 2 sts, sc in next tr; rep from * to end. Fasten off, leaving a tail at least 8" (20.5 cm) long. Do not turn work.

Row 3 (RS): With color A and leaving a tail at least 8" (20.5 cm) long, join yarn with a sl st in sc from beg of Row 2. Ch 4 (counts as first tr), tr and dc in same st, *sk 2 sts, sc in next tr, sk 2 sts, (dc, 3 tr, dc) in next sc, rep from * to ending last rep with (dc, 2tr) in last sc. Fasten off, leaving a tail at least 8" (20.5 cm) long. Do not turn work.

Rep Rows 2 and 3 three more times, ending with Row 3.

Fringe

1st Side: *Cut a 53" (134.5 cm) length of yarn of each color. Fold tog each strand in half, then in half again. Pull the looped end of the folded yarn through the end of the scarf from the RS to the WS. Pull the end of the tassel through the loop along with any adjacent ends dangling from the scarf and pull tight to secure; rep from * 5 more times— 6 tassels.

2nd Side: Rep as for 1st side.

Finishing

When all tassels are attached, trim ends to about 8" (20.5 cm) or desired length.

Weave remaining tail ends into tassel. Block scarf.

Finished Measurements
About 27¾ (30¼, 33¾, 35¾)" [70.5 (77, 85.5, 90.5) cm] circumference (buckled).

Yarn
DK weight (#3 Light).

Shown here: Knit Picks *CotLin DK* (70% tanguis cotton, 30% linen; 123 yd [113m]/50 g): Linen (MC), 1 (1, 2, 2) ball(s); Harbor (A), Moroccan Red (B), and Coffee (C), 1 ball each.

Hook
Size 5 (3.75 mm) Tunisian hook or size needed to obtain gauge.

Notions
MJtrim.com Faux Leather Buckle with Tabs, Style #42058, tan; sewing needle; matching thread of belt buckle; sewing pins; tapestry needle.

Gauge
18 sts and 18 rows = 4" (10 cm) in Tunisian simple stitch (Tss).

Take time to check gauge.

Embellished Belt

Top off a simple dress with this stunning belt and turn a basic outfit into a stylish statement! Tunisian crochet forms the base for this piece, making it perfectly sturdy and completely comfortable at the same time. The grid-like structure of Tunisian stitches is an ideal canvas for embroidery or cross-stitch—get creative and add your own spin to the embroidery, going as elaborate or minimal as you like.

❋ DESIGNED BY REGINA RIOUX ❋

Tss (Tunisian simple stitch)
(Worked in 2 passes to complete a row)

Forward Pass: Beg with a single loop on the hook from the prior row, sk 1st vertical bar, *insert hook in next vertical bar, yarn over, draw up loop; rep from * across leaving all loops on hook. Do not turn.

Return Pass: To complete row, yarn over, draw through 1 loop on hook, *yarn over, draw through 2 loops on hook; rep from * across until 1 loop remains on hook.

Inc 1: Insert hook under 2 horizontal strands bet 2 vertical bars, yo and draw up loop.

Dec 1: Insert hook from right to left into 2 vertical bars, yarn over and draw up loop through both vertical bars.

Backstitch: Bring the needle and thread from the back to the front of the fabric. Put the needle down through the fabric about ⅛" (3 mm) away from where you started.

Bring the needle up about ⅛" (3 mm) away from where you went down. Pull the thread through. Put the needle back down in the same spot you did before, taking a backstitch.

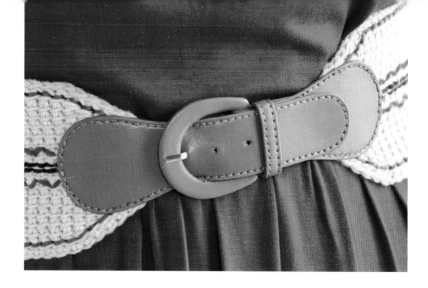

Instructions
Belt

With MC, ch 8.

Row 1 (Forward Pass): Draw up loop in back side loop beg in 2nd ch from hook and in each ch across—8 loops on hook, do not turn.

Row 1 and all rows on Return Pass: Yo, draw through 1 loop on hook, *yo, draw through 2 loops on hook; rep from * across—1 loop remains on hook (counts as 1st st on next row), do not turn.

Row 2 (Forward Pass): Inc 1 bet 1st and 2nd sts, Tss in each st to last st, Inc 1 bet last 2 sts, Tss in the 2 edge loops of last st—10 Tss, do not turn.

Rows 3–6: Repeat Inc Row 2—18 Tss.

Row 7 (Forward Pass): Tss in next and in each st across to last st, Tss in the 2 edge loops of last st, do not turn.

Rep Row 7 until piece measures 22 (24½, 28, 30) " [56 (62, 71, 76) cm] from beg.

Next Row (Forward Pass): Sk 1st st, Dec 1 over next 2 sts, Tss to last 3 sts, Dec 1 over next 2 sts, Tss in the two edge loops of last st—16 Tss, do not turn.

Rep last Dec Row 4 more times—8 Tss.

Last Row (Forward Pass only): Skip first vertical bar, *insert hook under next vertical bar, yo and draw through both loops on hook; rep from * across. Do not fasten off, ch 1, rotate work 45° to right.

Edging

Work 5 sl sts evenly along edge, rotate work 45° to right, ch 1, sl st in each st to end of long side (at point where the belt rows beg to Dec), ch 1, rotate work 45° to right, work 5 sl sts evenly along edge, ch 1, sl st in next st. Fasten off.

Finishing

Lay belt on surface with WS facing, fold ends about ⅓ toward middle. Position and pin buckle about 1½" (3.8 cm) from each end. With needle and thread, sew buckle to belt using existing holes in top stitching of buckle. Weave in remaining ends and embroider belt as detailed below.

Belt Embroidery

With colors A, B, and C, embroider the RS of the belt using backstitch, as shown in diagram.

Color Key
- ■ Harbor (A)
- ■ Moroccan Red (B)
- ■ Coffee (C)

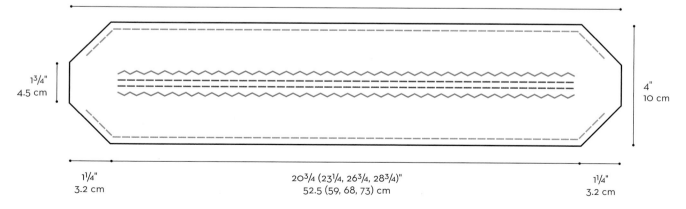

23¼ (25¾, 29¼, 31¼)"
59 (65.5, 74.5, 79.5) cm

1¾"
4.5 cm

4"
10 cm

1¼"
3.2 cm

20¾ (23¼, 26¾, 28¾)"
52.5 (59, 68, 73) cm

1¼"
3.2 cm

Finished Measurements

9½" (24 cm) long by 4½" (11.5 cm) wide.

Yarn

Worsted weight (#4 Medium).

Shown here: Cascade *220 Superwash* (100% superwash wool; 220 yd [200 m]/3.5 oz [100 g]): #841 Moss (A), #910A Winter White (B), #1910 Summer Sky Heather (C), #821 Daffodil (D), #893 Ruby (E), #807 Raspberry (F), 1 ball each.

Hook

Size H/8 (5 mm) or size needed to obtain gauge.

Notions

Six ⁷⁄₁₆" (11 mm) buttons; tapestry needle.

Gauge

16 sts and 11 rows = 4" (10 cm) in relief stitch pattern using size H/8 (5 mm) hook.

Take time to check gauge.

Stripey Mitts

Add some color to winter days with these bright and cheery mittens. Use your scrap yarn to work a random stripe sequence or keep it simple with fewer colors. Whether you make these mitts flamboyant or muted, their classic shape ensures that they will be the ones you reach for over and over again as you're heading out the door.

❈ DESIGNED BY ROBYN CHACHULA ❈

Front Loop Only (flo)

Back Loop Only (blo)

STITCH GUIDE

FPdc (Front Post double crochet)

Yarn over, insert hook around post of next indicated st by inserting hook from front to back to front around the post, yarn over and draw up loop, [yarn over and pull through 2 loops on hook] twice.

BPdc (Back Post double crochet)

Yarn over, insert hook around post of next indicated st by inserting hook from back to front to back around the post, yarn over and draw up loop, [yarn over and pull through 2 loops on hook] twice.

Dc#tog (Double crochet together)

*Yarn over, insert hook into next indicated st, yarn over and draw up loop, yarn over and pull yarn through 2 loops on hook; rep from * # times total, yarn over and pull through remaining loops on hook.

Relief Stitch Pattern (worked flat)
(Multiple of 5 sts + 2 + 2 ch)

Ch 19.

Row 1 (WS): Dc in 4th ch from hook and in each ch across—17 dc. Turn.

Row 2: Ch 3 (counts as dc), *[dc in next dc, FPdc around next dc] twice, dc in next dc; rep from * to last dc, dc in last dc. Turn.

Row 3: Ch 3 (counts as dc), *[dc in next dc, BPdc around next dc], dc in next dc; rep from * to last dc, dc in last dc. Turn.

Rep Rows 2 and 3.

NOTES

❀ Mittens are worked from the top down to the cuff with an opening for the thumb.

❀ Work in following stripe-row sequence throughout pattern: 1 Round A, 1 Round B, 1 Round C, 1 Round D, 1 Round E, 1 Round F.

Instructions

Right Mitten

Start stripe sequence and make an adjustable ring with A.

Rnd 1 (RS): Ch 3 (counts as dc), 11 dc in ring, pull ring closed, sl st to top of t-ch—12 dc, do not turn, fasten off A and join B.

Rnd 2: Ch 3 (counts as dc), *(dc, FPdc) in next dc, dc in next dc; rep from * around to last dc, (dc, FPdc) in last dc, sl st to top of t-ch—18 dc, do not turn.

Rnd 3: Ch 3 (counts as dc), *dc in next dc, 2 FPdc around next dc, dc in next dc; rep from * around to last 2 dc, dc in next dc, 2 FPdc around last dc, sl st to top of t-ch, do not turn—24 dc.

Rnd 4: Ch 3 (counts as dc), *dc in next dc, FPdc around next dc, dc bet FPdc, FPdc around next dc, dc in next dc; rep from * around to last 3 dc, dc in next dc, FPdc around next dc, dc bet FPdc, FPdc around last dc, sl st to top of t-ch, do not turn—30 dc.

Rnd 5: Ch 3 (counts as dc), *[dc in next dc, FPdc around next dc] twice, dc in next dc; rep from * around to last 4 dc, [dc in next dc, FPdc around next dc] twice, sl st to top of t-ch, do not turn.

Rnds 6–12: Rep Rnd 5.

THUMB OPENING

Rnd 13: Ch 3 (counts as dc), *[dc in next dc, FPdc around next dc] twice, dc in next dc; rep from * once, [dc in next dc, FPdc around next dc] twice, ch 7, skip 2 dc, **[FPdc around next dc, dc in next dc] twice, dc in next dc; rep from ** once, FPdc around next dc, dc in next dc, FPdc around last dc, sl st to top of t-ch, do not turn.

Rnd 14: Ch 3 (counts as dc), FPdc around each FPdc, dc in each dc and in each 7 ch; sl st to top of t-ch—35 dc, do not turn.

Rnds 15–17: Rep Rnd 5.

Rnd 18: Ch 3 (counts as dc), *dc in next dc, FPdc around next dc, skip next dc, FPdc around next dc, dc in next dc*, [dc in next dc, FPdc around next dc] twice, dc in next dc, rep from * to * 3 times, [dc in next dc, FPdc around next dc] twice, dc in next dc, dc in next dc, FPdc around next dc, skip next dc, FPdc around next dc, sl st to top of t-ch, do not turn, fasten off—30 dc.

RIGHT CUFF

Row 19 (RS): Skip 19 dc, join yarn with sl st in next FPdc, ch 3 (counts as dc), FPdc around next FPdc, dc flo in next 2 dc, [FPdc around next dc, dc in next dc] twice, [dc in next dc, FPdc around next 2 dc, dc in next dc] twice, [dc in next dc, FPdc around next dc] twice, dc in next dc, [dc in next dc, FPdc around next 2 dc, dc in next dc] twice, dc in next dc, dc blo in next 4 dc (overlap made)—34 dc, turn.

Rows 20 (WS), 22, and 24: Ch 3 (counts as dc), dc in each dc, BPdc in each FPdc around, turn.

Rows 21, 23, and 25: Ch 3 (counts as dc), FPdc around each FPdc, dc in each dc around, turn.

Row 26 (WS): Rep Row 20, fasten off.

EDGING

With RS facing, join C to outer side edge of cuff with sl st, ch 1, [2 sc in each row end] 8 times to corner, 3 sc in corner st, turn work 90°, sc in each dc around, 3 sc in last dc (for corner), turn work 90°, [2 sc in each row end] 8 times, fasten off.

BUTTONHOLE BAND

Join C to RS of outside edge of cuff with sl st, *sl st in next 4 sc, ch 3; rep from * twice more, sl st in each sc to end, fasten off, weave in ends.

Sew buttons to opposite cuff opening.

THUMB

With RS facing, join A in corner of thumb opening.

Rnd 1: Ch 3 (counts as dc), 12 dc evenly around opening—13 dc, sl st to top of t-ch, do not turn. Fasten off A.

Rnd 2: Join F, ch 3 (counts as dc), dc in each dc around, sl st to top of t-ch, do not turn. Fasten off F.

Rnd 3: Rep Rnd 2 with E.

Rnd 4: Join D, ch 3 (counts as dc), *dc2tog over next 2 dc, dc in next 2 dc; rep from * around, sl st to top of t-ch, fasten off D—10 dc.

Rnd 5: Join C, ch 2, [dc2tog over next 2 dc, dc3tog over next 3 dc] twice, sl st to first dc2tog, weave ends through top of sts and pull closed, fasten off.

Left Mitten

Rep as for right mitten to cuff.

LEFT CUFF

Row 19 (RS): Skip 8 dc, join yarn with sl st in next FPdc, ch 3 (counts as dc), dc blo in next 3 dc, [FPdc around next dc, dc in next 2 dc, FPdc around next dc] 3 times, dc in next dc, FPdc around next dc, dc in next 2 dc, [FPdc around next dc, dc in next 2 dc, FPdc around next dc] twice, dc in next dc, FPdc around next dc, dc flo in next 2 dc, FPdc around next dc (overlap made)—34 dc, turn.

Complete as for right mitten.

EDGING

With RS facing join C to inner side edge of cuff with sl st, ch 1, [2 sc in each row end] 8 times to corner, 3 sc in corner st, turn work 90°, sc in each dc around, 3 sc in last dc (for corner), turn work 90°, [2 sc in each row end] 8 times, fasten off.

BUTTONHOLE BAND

Work as for right mitten.

Finishing

Weave in all ends.

Size

Men's Small 21½"–21¾"
(54.5–55 cm), Medium
22"–22½" (56–57 cm), Large
23"–23¾" (58.5–60.5 cm).

Yarn

DK weight (#3 Light).

Shown here: Rowan *Wool
Cotton* (50% merino /50%
cotton; 123 yd [113 m]/50 g):
#965 Mocha, 3 balls.

Hook

Size E (3.5 mm) or size
needed to obtain gauge.

Size G (4.0 mm) and Size C
(2.75 mm).

Notions

Two coat buttons ⅝" (15 mm)
diameter with holes large
enough to sew with a small
yarn needle; split ring
or locking stitch marker;
tapestry needle.

Gauge

25 sts and 20 rnds = 4" (10 cm)
in linked stitch pattern using
size E (3.5 mm) hook.

Take time to check gauge.

Kings County Pork Pie Hat

This unique cap is inspired by the pork pie hat that was popular during the Jazz Age and lately has come back into style with full force. This modernized crochet version, worked in Tunisian crochet, is soft and flexible enough to be thrown in a tote bag, yet still structured enough to keep its shape during even the wildest jam session.

❊ **DESIGNED BY ANTONIO LIMUACO, THE YARN MONKEY** ❊

Lsc *(Linked single crochet)*
Insert hook through the vertical strand closest to the hook and through next st. Draw yarn through both (2 loops on the hook).

Ldc *(Linked double crochet)*
Insert hook through vertical strand closest to the hook and the top ch to its left. Draw yarn through both keeping new loop on the hook. Insert hook in next st and draw loop (3 loops on the hook). [Draw yarn through 2 loops] twice.

Ltc *(Linked treble crochet)*
*Insert hook through vertical strand closest to the hook and the top ch to its left. Draw yarn through both, keeping new loop on the hook; repeat from * once more in the next set. Insert hook in next st and draw loop (4 loops on the hook). [Draw yarn through 2 loops] 3 times.

Inc Lsc to Ldc
Insert hook through the vertical strand closest to the hook and draw a loop. Insert hook in next st and draw loop (3 loops on the hook). [Draw yarn through 2 loops] twice.

Inc Ldc to Ltc
Insert hook through the vertical strand closest to the hook and draw a loop. Then insert hook through the same strand and the top ch to its left and draw another loop through both. Insert hook in next st and draw loop (4 loops on the hook). [Draw yarn through 2 loops] 3 times.

Dec Ldc to Lsc
Insert hook through the vertical strand closest to the hook and through next st. Draw yarn through both keeping new loop on the hook (2 loops on the hook). Draw yarn through 2 loops.

Dec Ltc to Ldc
Insert hook through the 2 vertical strands. Draw yarn through both keeping new loop on the hook. Insert hook in next st and draw loop (3 loops on the hook). [Draw yarn through 2 loops] twice.

Instructions

Note: Rounds are worked in spiral. Place locking marker on first st to mark the beg of rounds and transfer marker to first st on each round as you work.

Crown *(make 2)*

With size E (3.5 mm) hook, make an adjustable ring and close with sl st.

Rnd 1 (RS): 10 sc into ring. Gently pull end to tighten ring.

Rnd 2: 1 sc, 2 lsc in the next st, inc lsc to ldc, 2 ldc in the next stitch, *1 ldc, 2 ldc in the next st; rep from * to end of rnd—15 sts.

Rnd 3: 2 ldc in each st to end of rnd—30 sts.

Rnd 4: *Ldc in next 2 sts, 2 ldc in next st; rep from to end of rnd—40 sts.

Rnd 5: Inc ldc to ltc, 1 ltc in next 2 sts, 2 ltc in next st, *ltc in next 3 sts, 2 ltc in next st; rep from * to end of rnd—50 sts.

Rnd 6: *Ltc in 1st st, 2 ltc in next st; rep from * to end of rnd—75 sts.

Rnd 7: *Ltc in next 4 sts, 2 ltc in next st; rep from * to end of rnd—90 sts.

Continue to instructions for small, medium, or large sizes.

FOR SIZE SMALL

Rnd 8: (Dec ltc to ldc) in 1st st, ldc in next 7 sts, 2 ltc in next st, *ldc in next 8 sts, 2 ldc in next st; rep from * 3 more times, (dec ldc to lsc) in next st, lsc in the next 7 sts, 2 lsc in next st, *lsc in next 8 sts, 2 lsc in next st; rep from * 3 more times—100 sts.

FOR SIZE MEDIUM

Rnd 8: (Dec ltc to ldc) in 1st st, ldc in next 4 sts, 2 ltc in next st, *ldc in next 5 sts, 2 ldc in next st; rep from * 5 more times, (dec ldc to lsc) in next st, lsc in the next 4 sts, 2 lsc in next st, *lsc in next 5 sts, 2 lsc in next st; rep from * 6 more times—105 sts.

FOR SIZE LARGE

Rnd 8: *Ltc in next 8 sts, 2 ltc in next st; rep from * to end of rnd—100 sts.

Rnd 9: (Dec ltc to ldc) in 1st st, ldc in next 8 sts, 2 ltc in next st, *ldc in next 9 sts, 2 ldc in next st; rep from * 3 more times, (dec ldc to lsc) in next st, lsc in the next 8 sts, 2 lsc in next st, *lsc in next 9 sts, 2 lsc in next st; rep from * 3 more times—110 sts.

Set 1st circular panel aside. Fasten off.

Make 2nd circular panel as for 1st panel; do not fasten off.

With WS tog, match edges of both panels. Join together with loose slip stitch around edge between posts—100 (105, 110) sts. Do not fasten off.

Change to size G (4.0 mm) hook.

Welt

Rnd 1: Sc in each ch of the sl st seam to end of rnd—100 (105, 110) sts.

Rnds 2 and 3: Sc in each st to end of rnd.

Rnds 4 and 5: Sl st in each st to end of rnd.

Rnds 6 and 7: Sc in each st to end of rnd.

Fold welt to join with the outer edge crown.

Rnd 8: Sc in each st through both layers to end of rnd—100 (105, 110) sts. Do not fasten off.

Change to size E (3.5 mm) hook.

Side Band

Rnd 1: Sc in 1st st, lsc in next 3 sts, (inc lsc to ldc) in next st, ldc in next (47, 49, 52) sts, (inc ldc to ltc) in next st, ltc to end of rnd—100, 105, 110 sts.

Rnds 2–4: Ltc in each st to end of rnd.

Rnd 5: Ltc in next (49, 52, 54) sts, (dec ltc to ldc) in next st, ldc in each st to last 5 sts, then (dec ldc to lsc) in next st, lsc in next 3 sts, sl st in last st. Do not fasten off.

Change to size G (4.0 mm) hook.

Brim

Rnd 1 (RS): Sl st loosely between posts around edge of side band—100, 105, 110 sts.

Rnd 2: Sl st in 1st st, sc in next 3 sts, 2 sc in next st, *sc in next 4 sts, 2 sc in next st; rep from * to end of rnd—120, 126, 132.

Change to size E (3.5 mm) hook.

Rnd 3: Sc in 1st st, lsc in next 3 sts, (inc lsc to ldc) in next st, ldc in next (54, 57, 60) sts, (inc ldc to ltc) in next st, ltc in each st to end of rnd.

Rnd 4: *Ltc in next (19, 20, 21) sts, 2 ltc in next st; rep from * to end of rnd—126, 132, 138 sts.

Rnd 5: [Ltc in next (20, 21, 22) sts, 2 ltc in next st] twice, (dec ltc to ldc) in next st, ldc in next (19, 20, 21) sts, 2 ldc in next st, ldc in next (20, 21, 22) sts, 2 ldc in next st, (dec ldc to lsc) in next st, lsc in next (19, 20, 21) sts, 2 lsc in next st, lsc in next (20, 21, 22) sts, 2 lsc in next st—132, 138, 144. Do not fasten off.

Change to size C (2.75 mm) hook.

Trim the Brim

Rnd 6: Sc in each st to end of rnd—132, 138, 144.

Rnd 7: Sl st between posts of prev Rnd 6 to end of rnd. Turn.

Rnd 8 (WS): Sl st between posts of Rnd 6 to end. Fasten off, weaving end through first st following the chain pattern. Weave in ends.

Trim Top of Welt

With RS facing and with size C (2.75 mm) hook, work through the bar between Rnds 3 and 4 of the fold edge of welt (this is the row above the two slipped rows; start 3 or 4 sts away from the point of origin where rnds meet imperfectly) as folls:

Rnd 1: Sl st in first st, sc in each st to end of rnd— 100, 105, 110 sts. Do not join rnd.

Rnd 2: Sl st between posts of rnd 1 to end of rnd. Turn.

Rnd 3 (RS): Sl st between posts of Rnd 1 to end. Fasten off weaving tail through first st of rnd foll chain pattern. Weave in ends.

Trim Side of Welt

With size E (3.5 mm) hook, locate rnd 1 of side band on the RS of the hat (this is the raised stitch where welt meets the side band). With RS of crown facing up, beg 3 or 4 sts away from the point of origin (where rounds meet imperfectly). Insert hook through the bottom of raised stitch and sl st to end of rnd. Fasten off, weaving tail through first st of rnd following chain pattern. Sew in ends.

Trim Inside Band

Note: For a closer fit, use size C (2.75 mm) hook.

With size E (3.5 mm) hook, locate the ch st seam where the side band meets the brim on the WS. With WS facing you, beg 3 or 4 sts away from the point of origin (where rnds meet imperfectly) and sl st to end of rnd. Fasten off, weaving tail through first st of rnd foll chain pattern. Weave in ends.

Finishing

Machine wash on gentle cycle in cold water. Gently remove excess water by laying hat on a dry absorbent towel and roll up in the towel, pressing firmly as you roll. Do not wring towel. Lay flat to dry. Iron lightly with spray starch to keep it crisp.

Optional Hatband with Band Loops

THE BAND LOOPS (MAKE 2)

With size E (3.5 mm) hook, ch 7.

Row 1: Sc in 2nd ch from hook and in each ch to end—6 sc. Turn.

Rows 2–6: Ch 1, sc in each sc. Turn.

EDGING

*Sl st between posts on long side—6 sl sts, ch 1, sl st in next 5 sc, ch 1; rep from * once more to end. Fasten off, leaving 6" (15 cm) tail for sewing.

THE HATBAND

(22, 23, 24) " [(56. 58.5, 61) cm]

With size E (3.5 mm) hook, ch 111, 116, 121.

Rnd 1: 2 sc in 2nd ch from hook, 2 sc in next ch, sc in each ch to last 2 ch, 2 sc in each of last 2 ch. Cont to other side of fnd ch, 2 sc in each of first 2 ch, sc in each ch to last 2 ch, 2 sc in each of last 2 ch—118, 123, 128, sts.

Rnd 2: Sl st in top of each sc.

Rnd 3: Sl st in top of each sc from prev row. Join with sl st. Do not fasten off.

BUTTON LOOP

Change to size C (2.75 mm) hook and ch 10. Join with sl st to 1st ch.

Rnd 4: Sl st in each ch around, fasten off, sew in ends.

Wash straps and belt, air-dry flat.

ASSEMBLE AND SEW THE BAND LOOPS

With RS facing, sew bottom of band loop to seam where brim meets the side band using whipstitch. Sew top of band loop to side band leaving enough room to insert hat band through. In the same manner, sew second band loop directly on opppsite side of side band.

ASSEMBLE AND SEW THE HATBAND

With RS facing, sew first button to end of hatband before button loop. Sew 2nd button about ¾" (2 cm) from opposite end of hatband. Position this end of hatband about ½" (1.3 cm) from right side of a band loop and sew to side band using whipstitch. Insert button loop end of hatband counterclockwise through opposite band loop, then into 1st band loop to close button.

Size
One size.

Finished Measurements
10" (25 cm) length by 24" (61 cm) circumference.

Yarn
Worsted weight (#4 Medium).

Shown here: Caron *Stitch. Rock.Love Sheep(ish),* (70% acrylic, 30% wool; 167 yd [153 m]/3 oz [85 g]): #0016 Teal(ish), 2 balls.

Hook
Size J (5.5 mm) or size needed to obtain gauge.

Notions
Tapestry needle.

Gauge
14¼ sts and 4½ rows = 4" (10 cm) in V-st patt using size J (5.5 mm) hook.

Take time to check gauge.

Cozy Cowl

This simple neck warmer is just the thing to take the edge off on a chilly fall day. It's versatile enough to be worn over a denim jacket or a wool coat—and best of all, you can complete it in just an afternoon.

❊ **DESIGNED BY VICKIE HOWELL** ❊

Instructions

Body

Ch 28.

Row 1: Dc in 3rd ch from hook (ch 3 counts as dc), skip 2 ch, *[dc, ch, dc] in next ch, skip 2 ch; rep from * ending with 2 dc in last ch—18 dc and 7 ch-1 sps. Turn.

Row 2: Ch 3, dc in front loop of same st as ch 3, skip 2 dc, *3 dc in front loop of ch-sp, skip 2 dc; rep from * ending with 2 dc in front loop of last dc. Turn.

Row 3: Ch 3, dc in *front loop* of same st as ch 3, skip 2 dc, *[dc, ch, dc] in *front loop* of next dc (this will be the middle of the 3-dc group from the prev row), skip 2 dc; rep from * ending with 2 dc in last st. Turn.

Repeat Rows 2 and 3 until piece measures 24" (61 cm) from beg. Fasten off; set aside.

Ribbed Bands *(make 2)*

Ch 8.

Row 1 (WS): Sc in 2nd ch from hook and to end—7 sc. Turn.

Row 2: Ch 1, sc in front loop of 1st sc and in front loop of each sc to end. Turn.

Row 3: Ch 1, sc in unworked *back loop* of first sc of row below, and each unworked *back loop* to end. Turn.

Rows 4 and 5: Ch 1, sc in each stitch across. Turn.

Rep Rows 2–5 until band measures 24" (61 cm) from beg. Fasten off.

Finishing

Sew bands to top and bottom of long sides of body piece. Sew seam of short side together to form tube. Weave in ends.

Finished Measurements
6" (15 cm) wide (at widest point) by 6" (15 cm) high.

Yarn
DK weight (#3 Light).

Shown here: Classic Elite *Magnolia*, (70% merino, 30% silk, 120 yd [110 m]/50 g): #5475 Granite (MC), #5415 Pale Teal (A), #5435 Citron (B), 1 skein each.

Hook
Size F (3.75 mm) or size needed to obtain gauge.

Notions
Inazuma Purse Frame #BK-1275, 4¾" × 3¼" (12 cm × 8.5 cm); tapestry needle.

Gauge
16 sts and 18 rows = 4" (10 cm) in sc stitch using size F (3.75 mm) hook.

Take time to check gauge.

Flowering Change Purse

A charming hinged frame takes this little purse from simple to special. It's a perfect catch-all for anything from spare change to makeup. Make as many as you wish; they can even hold your buttons and notions! This purse makes a great gift for girlfriends of all ages.

❋ DESIGNED BY AMY POLCYN ❋

STITCH GUIDE

Sc2tog (Single crochet 2 together)
Insert hook in next stitch, yarn over and pull up loop (2 loops on hook), insert hook in next stitch, yarn over and pull up loop (3 loops on hook), yarn over and draw through all 3 loops on hook.

Tr (Treble crochet)
*Yarn over 2 times, insert hook in stitch, yarn over and pull up loop (4 loops on hook), yarn over and draw through 2 loops, yarn over and draw through 2 loops, yarn over and draw through remaining 2 loops; repeat from *.

Dtr (Double treble crochet)
Yarn over 3 times, insert hook in stitch, yarn over and pull up loop, [yarn over, draw through 2 loops on hook] 4 times.

Instructions

Panel (make 2)

With MC, ch 17.

Row 1 (RS): Sc in 2nd ch from hook and each ch across—16 sc. Turn.

Row 2: Ch 1, sc in each sc across. Turn.

Rep Row 2 until piece measures 1" (2.5 cm) from beg.

Next (inc) row: Ch 1, 2 sc in first sc, sc in each sc across to last sc, 2 sc in last sc—18 sc. Turn.

Next row: Ch 1, sc in each sc across. Turn.

Rep last row until piece measures 2" (5 cm) from beg.

Rep inc row every other row 3 times—24 sts.

Work even in sc for 4 rows.

Next (dec) row: Ch 1, sc2tog, sc in each sc to last 2 sc, sc2tog—22 sc. Turn.

Rep dec row every other row 2 more times—18 sc.

Next row: Ch 1, *sc2tog; rep from * across—9 sc. Fasten off.

Flower (make 2)

With B, ch 5. Join with a sl st to form a ring.

Rnd 1: Ch 1, work 10 sc in ring, join with a sl st in first sc. Do not turn.

Rnd 2: Ch 1, sc in each sc around, join with a sl st in first sc. Do not turn.

Rnd 3: Ch 2 (counts as hdc), work 2 hdc in next 9 sc, hdc in same sc as ch 2, join with sl st to ch 2—20 hdc. Do not turn. Fasten off.

Rnd 4: Join A with a sl st in *front loop* of any hdc. *Ch 2, *working in front loops only,* 2 hdc in each of next 3 hdc, ch 2, sl st in next hdc; rep from * around, join with a sl st in first sl st—5 petals. Do not turn.

Rnd 5: Working in back loops only of Rnd 3, sl st in first hdc, *ch 4, 2 dtr in each of the next 3 hdc (behind petal), ch 4, sl st in next hdc; rep from * around, ending with ch 4 and join with a sl st in first sl st—5 petals. Fasten off.

Flower Centers *(make 2)*

With MC, ch 5. Join with a sl st to form a ring.

Rnd 1: Ch 1, work 10 sc in ring, join with a sl st in first sc. Fasten off.

Leaves *(make 2)*

With C, ch 11.

Rnd 1: Working in top edge of ch, sc in 2nd ch from hook, sc in next ch, hdc in next 2 ch, dc in next 2 ch, tr in next ch, dc in next ch, hdc in next ch, 3 sc in last ch. Continuing on opposite edge of ch, work hdc in next ch, dc in next ch, tr in next ch, dc in next 2 ch, hdc in next 2 ch, sc in next 2 ch, join with sl st to first sc. Fasten off.

Finishing

Sew flower centers to flowers. Place 1 flower on each side of bag and sew in place around inner edge of petals. Arrange 2 leaves on each side of bag and sew in place down center of each leaf.

Put WS of front and back tog. With MC, work a row of sc around outside edges of bag, working through both layers leaving 2" (5 cm) top for opening. Fasten off. Weave in ends.

Attach purse frame following manufacturer's instructions.

Finished Measurements

11" (28 cm) wide by 5½" (14 cm) high, *before felting.*

8" (20.5 cm) wide by 4¾" (12 cm) high, *after felting.*

Motif A = 4" (10 cm) diameter.

Motif B = 2¾" (7 cm) diameter.

Yarn

DK weight (#3 Light).

Shown here: Blue Sky Alpaca *Suri Merino* (60% baby suri alpaca, 40% merino wool; 164 yd [150 m]/3.5 oz [100 g]): #423 Twilight (MC), #417 Seamist (A), #420 Autumn (B), 1 hank each.

Hook

Size H/8 (5 mm) or size needed to obtain gauge.

Notions

Needlefelting pad and pen; 8" (20.5 cm) all-purpose zipper matching MC; tapestry needle; sewing thread of matching MC; sewing needle.

Gauge

16 sts and 11 rows = 4" (10 cm) in hdc stitch patt using H/8 (5 mm) hook.

Take time to check gauge.

Mixed-Motif Clutch

This sweet little clutch is created using two special techniques: first the body is wet-felted and then it is embellished with motifs that are attached by needle felting. The result is both beautiful and functional, and it's guaranteed to have folks asking, "How did you do that?"

❊ **DESIGNED BY ROBYN CHACHULA** ❊

Tr

*Yarn over 2 times, insert hook in st, yarn over and pull up loop (4 loops on hook), yarn over and draw through 2 loops, yarn over and draw through 2 loops, yarn over and draw through remaining 2 loops; rep from *.

Dtr

Yarn over 3 times, insert hook in stitch, yarn over and pull up loop, [yarn over, draw through 2 loops on hook] 4 times.

P-st

Dtr in st indicated, ch 4, dc in middle of prev dtr post.

Y-st

Tr in st indicated, ch 4, hdc in middle of prev tr post.

Picot

Ch 3, sl st to first ch.

NOTES ....

❀ Clutch is crocheted and seamed before felting.

❀ Motifs are needlefelted onto clutch after.

Instructions

Ch 13 with MC.

Rnd 1 (RS): Hdc in 4th ch from hook (skip ch counts as hdc), hdc in each ch across to last, 5 hdc in last ch, turn 180 and begin working in free loops of foundation ch, hdc in next 9 ch, 4 hdc in next ch, sl st to first ch—28 hdc. Turn.

Rnd 2: Ch 2 (counts as hdc), hdc in top of t-ch, 2 hdc in next 4 hdc, hdc in next 9 hdc, 2 hdc in next 5 hdc, hdc in next 9 hdc, sl st to top of t-ch—38 hdc. Turn.

Rnd 3: Ch 2 (counts as hdc), hdc in next 9 hdc, [2 hdc in next hdc, hdc in next hdc] 5 times, hdc in next 9 hdc, [2 hdc in next hdc, hdc in next hdc] 4 times, 2 hdc in last hdc, sl st to top of t-ch—48 hdc. Turn.

Rnd 4: Ch 2 (counts as hdc), hdc in top of t-ch, hdc in next 2 hdc, [2 hdc in next hdc, hdc in next 2 hdc] 4 times, hdc in next 9 hdc, [2 hdc in next hdc, hdc in next 2 hdc] 5 times, hdc in next 9 hdc, sl st to top of t-ch—58 hdc. Turn.

Rnd 5: Ch 2 (counts as hdc), hdc in next 9 hdc, [2 hdc in next hdc, hdc in next 3 hdc] 5 times, hdc in next 9 hdc, [2 hdc in next hdc, hdc in next 3 hdc] 4 times, 2 hdc in next hdc, hdc in last 2 hdc, sl st to top of t-ch—68 hdc. Turn.

Rnd 6: Ch 2 (counts as hdc), hdc in top of t-ch, hdc in next 4 hdc, [2 hdc in next hdc, hdc in next 4 hdc] 4 times, hdc in next 9 hdc, [2 hdc in next hdc, hdc in next 4 hdc] 5 times, hdc in next 9 hdc, sl st to top of t-ch—78 hdc. Turn.

Rnd 7: Ch 2 (counts as hdc), hdc in next 9 hdc, [2 hdc in next hdc, hdc in next 5 hdc] 5 times, hdc in next 9 hdc, [2 hdc in next hdc, hdc in next 5 hdc] 4 times, 2 hdc in next hdc, hdc in last 4 hdc, sl st to top of t-ch—88 hdc. Turn.

Rnd 8: Ch 2 (counts as hdc), hdc in top of t-ch, hdc in next 6 hdc, [2 hdc in next hdc, hdc in next 6 hdc] 4 times, hdc in next 9 hdc, [2 hdc in next hdc, hdc in next 6 hdc] 5 times, hdc in next 9 hdc, sl st to top of t-ch—98 hdc. Turn.

Rnd 9: Ch 2 (counts as hdc), hdc in next 15 hdc, *[2 hdc in next hdc, hdc in next 6 hdc] twice, 2 hdc in next hdc, hdc in next 5 hdc, 2 hdc in next hdc, hdc in next 6 hdc, 2 hdc in next hdc*, hdc in next 21 hdc; rep from * to *, hdc in each hdc to end of rnd, sl st to top of t-ch—108 hdc. Turn.

Rnd 10: Ch 2 (counts as hdc), hdc in next 7 hdc, 2 hdc in next hdc, hdc in next 8 hdc, 2 hdc in next hdc, hdc in next 9 hdc, 2 hdc in next hdc, hdc in next 8 hdc, 2hdc in next hdc, hdc in next 25 hdc, 2 hdc in next hdc, hdc in next 8 hdc, 2 hdc in next hdc, hdc in next 9 hdc, 2 hdc in next hdc, hdc in next 8 hdc, 2 hdc in next hdc, hdc in each hdc to end of rnd, sl st to top of t-ch—116 hdc. Turn.

Rnd 11: Ch 2 (counts as hdc), hdc in each hdc around, sl st to top of t-ch. Turn.

Rnd 12: Ch 2 (counts as hdc), hdc in next 8 hdc, [2 hdc in next hdc, hdc in next 9 hdc] 4 times, hdc in next 18 hdc, [2 hdc in next hdc, hdc in next 9 hdc] 4 times, hdc in each hdc to end of rnd, sl st to top of t-ch—124 hdc. Turn.

Rnd 13: Ch 2 (counts as hdc), hdc in each hdc across, sl st to top of t-ch. Turn.

Rnd 14: Ch 2 (counts as hdc), hdc in next 9 hdc, 2 hdc in next hdc, hdc in next 10 hdc, 2 hdc in next hdc, hdc in next 9 hdc, 2 hdc in next hdc, hdc in next 10 hdc, 2hdc in next hdc, hdc in next 29 hdc, 2 hdc in next hdc, hdc in next 10 hdc, 2 hdc in next hdc, hdc in next 9 hdc, 2 hdc in next hdc, hdc in next 10 hdc, 2 hdc in next hdc, hdc in each hdc to end of rnd, sl st to top of t-ch—132 hdc. Turn.

Rnd 15: Ch 2 (counts as hdc), hdc in next 27 hdc, [2 hdc in next hdc, hdc in next 9 hdc] twice, 2 hdc in next hdc, hdc in next 45 hdc, [2 hdc in next hdc, hdc in next 9 hdc] twice, 2 hdc in next hdc, hdc in each hdc across, sl st to top of t-ch—138 hdc. Do not turn.

Side Flap

Row 1: Sl st to next hdc, ch 2 (counts as hdc), hdc in next 8 hdc—9 hdc. Turn.

Row 2: Ch 2 (counts as hdc), hdc in each hdc across. Turn.

Rep Row 2 eight times. Fasten off.

Opposite Flap

Row 1: Skip 60 hdc, join MC to next st with sl st, ch 2 (counts as hdc), hdc in next 8 hdc, turn.

Row 2: Ch 2 (counts as hdc), hdc in each hdc across. Turn.

Rep Row 2 eight times. Fasten off.

Seaming and Felting

Whipstitch body and flap edges together to form purse. Place clutch in bucket filled with hot water. Scrub clutch by hand for a few minutes, run clutch under cool water. Repeat hot scrubbing and cool

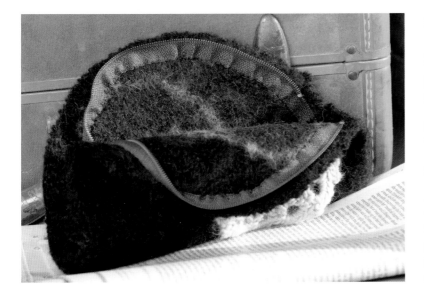

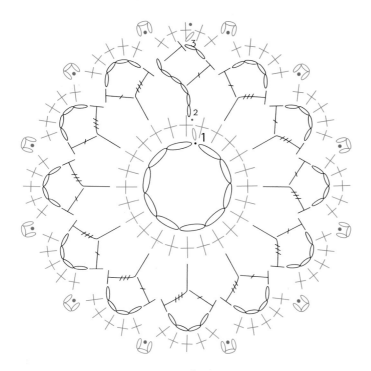
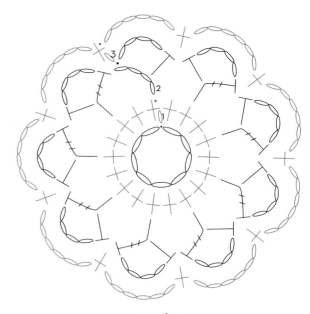

Motif A

Motif B

Stitch Key

⬭	chain (ch)	double treble crochet (dtr)	
•	slip st (sl st)	picot	
+	single crochet (sc)	P-st	
T	half double crochet (hdc)	Y-st	
⊤	double crochet (dc)		
⊤	treble crochet (tr)		

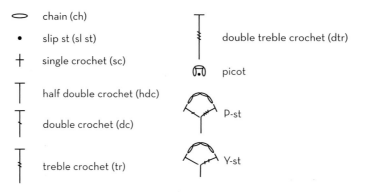

rinse until clutch is desired size. Place clutch over small box wrapped in plastic to dry.

Motif A *(make 2)*

Ch 10 with A, sl st to first ch to form ring. Do not turn.

Rnd 1: Ch 1, 24 sc in ring, sl st to first sc. Do not turn.

Rnd 2: Ch 6, [skip 1 sc, P-st in next st] 11 times, skip 1 sc, dc in 3rd ch of t-ch, ch 2, hdc in top of t-ch—12 p-sts. Do not turn.

Rnd 3: Ch 1, 3 sc around post of hdc, [picot, 5 sc in next ch-4 sp] 11 times, picot, 2 sc in first ch-2 sp. Fasten off and weave in ends.

Motif B *(make 2)*

Ch 9 with B, sl st to first ch to form ring. Do not turn.

Rnd 1: Ch 1, 18 sc in ring, sl st to first sc. Do not turn.

Rnd 2: Ch 4, [skip 1 sc, y-st in next st] 8 times, hdc in 2nd ch of t-ch, ch 4, sl st in top of t-ch—9 y-sts. Do not turn.

Rnd 3: Ch 1, sc bet t-ch and next y-st, [ch 6, sc bet y-sts] 8 times, ch 6, sl st to first sc. Fasten off and weave in ends.

Finishing

Using photo as guide, needlefelt motifs A and B to both sides of clutch.

Sew zipper to inside of bag, near the top edge.

Finished Measurements

Large Leaf: 3" (7.5 cm) long by 1¾" (4.5 cm) wide.

Small Leaf: 2¼" (5.5 cm) long by 1¼" (3 cm) wide.

Center Flower: 2¼" (5.5 cm) diameter.

Outer Ruffled Flower: 3" (7.5 cm) diameter.

Yarn

Chunky weight (#5 Bulky).

Shown here: Alchemy Yarns of Transformation *Mysterioso* (69% silk, 25% mohair, 6% wool; 115 yd [105 m]/50 g): #50E Sour Grass (A), #130W Blue Moon (B), #36F Lantern (C), and #38A Foxglove (D), 1 skein each.

Hook

Size H (5 mm) or size needed to obtain gauge.

Notions

Stitch marker (optional); tapestry needle; brooch pin fasteners; hot glue gun.

Gauge

16 sts = 4" (10 cm) in dc stitch using size H (5 mm) hook.

Take time to check gauge.

Chunky Flower Brooch

Brighten up almost anything with these crochet blossoms. Each one takes just minutes to stitch, and they're the perfect embellishment for a winter coat, hat, tote—or any piece that needs a little crafty flair. Wear them one at a time or cluster them for a veritable bouquet of color.

❖ DESIGNED BY FAITH HALE ❖

Instructions

Large Leaf

Ch 10 with A.

Rnd 1: Sc in 2nd ch from hook, hdc in next 2 ch, dc in next 2 ch, tr in next 3 ch, 8 tr in 1st ch. Turn leaf and work into the back of chain, tr in next 3 ch, dc in next 2 ch, hdc in next 2 ch, sc in last ch. Join with sl st to 1st sc. Fasten off.

Small Leaf

Ch 7 with A.

Rnd 1: Sc in 2nd ch from hook, hdc in next 2 ch, dc in next 2 ch, 6 dc in 1st ch. Turn leaf and work into the back of chain, dc in next 2 ch, hdc in next 2 ch, sc in last ch. Join with sl st in 1st sc. Fasten off.

Center Flower

Note: Rounds are worked in spiral; do not join at end of rnds. You may wish to place a marker for beg of rnd and move marker up as work progresses.

Ch 3, join with sl st to 1st sc.

Rnd 1: 6 sc in loop. Do not turn.

Rnd 2: 2 sc in each sc around—12sc. Do not turn. Fasten off. Attach contrasting color with sl st.

Rnd 3: Ch 4 (counts as sc and ch 3), *skip next sc, sc in next sc, ch 3; rep from * around. Do not turn.

Rnd 4: *Sc, 3 hdc, sc in ch-3 sp; rep from * around. Do not turn. Fasten off. Reattach contrasting color at an unworked sc of the initial color using a sl st.

Rnd 5: In the sc, work *1 sc, 3 hdc, 1 sc; rep from * around in each unworked sc from Rnd 3. Fasten off.

Outer Ruffled Flower

Note: Rounds are worked in spiral; do not join at end of rnds. You may wish to place a marker for beg of rnd and move marker up as work progresses.

Ch 3, join with sl st to 1st sc.

Rnd 1: 6 sc in loop. Do not turn.

Rnd 2: 2 sc in each sc around—12 sc. Do not turn.

Rnd 3: *Sc next sc, 2 sc in next sc; rep from * around—18 sc. Do not turn.

Rnd 4: *Sc in next sc, ch 4, sl st in 2nd, 3rd and 4th ch from hook, sl st into first sc worked; rep from * around—18 ruffles.

Finishing

Place center flower on outer ruffled flower and sew together. Sew leaves in back. Glue brooch pin fastener to back. Weave in all ends.

Finished Measurements

10" (25.5 cm) long and 14¼" (37 cm) high.

Yarn

DK weight (#3 Light).

Shown here: Rowan *Pure Wool DK*, (100% wool; 137 yd [125 m]/50 g): #004 Black (1), #007 Cypress (2), #008 Marine (3), #013 Enamel (4), #019 Avocado (5), #030 Damson (6), #042 Dahlia (7), 1 ball each; #003 Anthracite (8), 2 balls.

Hook

Size G (4 mm) or size needed to obtain gauge.

Notions

Leather purse handles, 16" (40.5 cm) long, 1 pair; tapestry needle; sewing thread, matching color to purse handles; sewing needle.

Gauge

One Flower Motif = 2" (5 cm) diameter using size G (4 mm) hook.

Take time to check gauge.

Amazing Motif Bag

Tiny textured flower motifs make up this gorgeous bag that's bursting with color and style. Sweet handles add the perfect touch, elevating this tote to a true work of art. Use your imagination to re-create this bag in the colorway of your dreams.

❉ **DESIGNED BY REGINA RIOUX** ❉

STITCH GUIDE

Tr4tog *(Treble crochet 4 together)*
*[Yarn over] twice, insert hook in indicated st and draw up a loop, [yarn over and draw through 2 loops] twice; repeat from * 3 more times, yarn over and draw through all 5 loops on hook.

Instructions

(Make 14 in each color: Black, Cypress, Marine, Enamel, Avocado, Damson.)

(Make 13 in each color: Dahlia and Anthracite.)

Flower Motif

Ch 2.

Rnd 1 (RS): 6 sc in first ch, join with sl st to first sc. Do not turn.

Rnd 2: (Ch 3, tr4tog, ch 3, sl st) in first sc, *[sl st, ch 3, tr4tog, ch 3, sl st) in next sc; rep from * 4 more times, join with sl st to base of beg ch 3. Fasten off.

Assembly

Lay motifs according to placement diagram with 2 petals from each motif adjacent to one another.

Joining Motifs *(make rows)*

Put RS of 2 motifs tog, *attach gray yarn at right edge, 1 sc through tops of 1st petal, 1 sc through sides of 1st petal, 1 sc through sides of 2nd petal, 1 sc through tops of 2nd petal—4 sc for seam, fasten off; rep from * for rem motifs to complete row. Lay stripes according to placement diagram.

Joining Rows

Put RS of 2 stripes together and attach gray yarn at right edge, *1 sc through tops of 1st petal, 1 sc

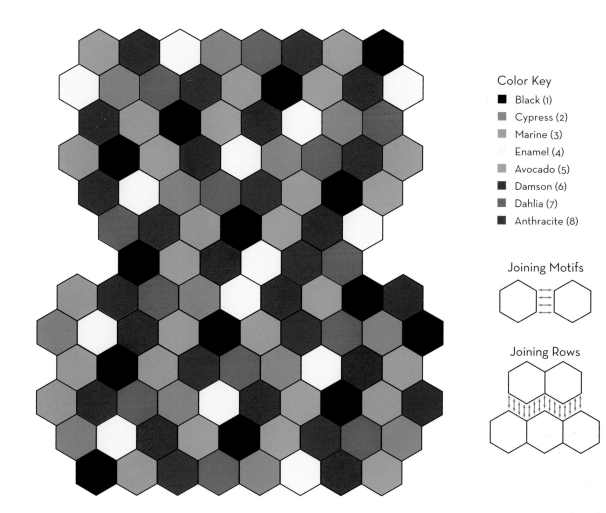

Color Key
- ■ Black (1)
- ■ Cypress (2)
- ■ Marine (3)
- □ Enamel (4)
- ■ Avocado (5)
- ■ Damson (6)
- ■ Dahlia (7)
- ■ Anthracite (8)

Joining Motifs

Joining Rows

through sides of 1st petal, 1 sc through sides of 2nd petal, 1 sc through sides of 2nd petal; rep from * for each side to end of stripe. Rep for rem stripes and side seams.

JOINING SIDE SEAMS
Rep as for joining rows for each side.

Finishing
Weave in all ends.

ASSEMBLE HANDLES
Position each end of handle between the 2nd and 3rd motifs from each side of the bag seam and 2nd row down from the top edge of bag. With sewing needle and thread, sew ends to bag.

Finished Measurements
2½" (6.5 cm) long by 1½" (4 cm) wide.

Yarn
Sport weight (#2 Fine).

Shown here: Habu A60 *Shosenshi* (100% linen paper; 280 yd [256 m]/2 oz): #113 Brick, 1 hank.

Hook
Size D (3 mm) or size needed to obtain gauge.

Notions
Silver fishhook earring wires, 1 pair; needle-nose pliers.

Gauge
7 sts = 1" (2.5 cm) in dc stitch using 2 strands tog and size D (3 mm) hook.

Take time to check gauge.

Drop Leaf Earrings

Tape yarn made of linen paper makes these simple earrings simply stunning. You can stitch each one in mere moments, making these a perfect small gift or a great last-minute accessory to add just the right handmade touch to your outfit.

❊ **DESIGNED BY KAZEKOBO** ❊

Instructions

Leaf (make 2)

Using 2 strands tog, ch 16.

Rnd 1: Sc in second ch from hook, hdc in next 2 ch, dc in next 2 ch, hdc in next 3 ch, sc in next 3 ch, ch 1, leave rem 4 ch unworked, turn to work on opposite side, sc in 3 ch, hdc in next 3 ch, dc in next 2 ch, hdc in next 2 ch, sc in last ch, ch 1, sl st in 1st sc on opposite side.

Rnd 2: Ch 2, hdc in next 2 hdc, [2 dc in next dc] twice, 2 dc in next hdc, hdc in next 2 hdc, hdc in next sc, sc in next 2 sc, sc in last 4 unworked fnd chs, ch 1, turn to work on opposite side, sl st in first 3 ch, sc in next ch, sc in next 2 sc, hdc in next sc, hdc in next 2 hdc, 2 dc in next hdc, [2 dc in next dc] twice, hdc in next 2 hdc, ch 2, skip 1 sc, sl st in ch-1 sp. Do not turn. Fasten off 1 strand.

Rnd 3: With 1 strand, ch 1, sl st in ch-2 sp, sl st in each st to tip, ch 1, turn to work on opposite side, sl st in each st to end of Rnd 2, ch 1, sl st in beg ch-1 sp. Fasten off.

Weave in ends.

Assembly

Open ear-wire loop with pliers by twisting loop open, not pulling loop apart. Hang base of leaf on ear-wire loop. Twist loop closed.

Rep for second earring.

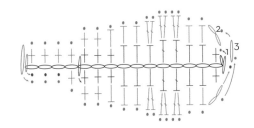

Chart Key

⌒ chain (ch)

• slip st (sl st)

✝ single crochet (sc)

⊤ half double crochet (hdc)

Ŧ double crochet (dc)

Size
To fit average men's shoe sizes 8–12.

Finished Measurements
Length: about 10" (25.5 cm).

Circumference: about 8" (20.5 cm).

Yarn
Sock weight (#1 Super Fine).

Shown here: Cascade *Heritage Silk* (85% merino superwash wool, 15% Mulberry Silk; 437 yd [400 m]/ 3.5 oz [100 g]): #5608 Pine, 3 hanks.

Hook
Size 3 (2.1 mm) steel hook or size needed to obtain gauge.

Notions
Stitch markers; tapestry needle.

Gauge
38 sts and 40 rnds = 4" (10 cm) in sc stitch using size 3 (2.1 mm) steel hook.

Take time to check gauge.

Hiking Socks

These heavy, sturdy socks are just the thing to wear under boots on a cold day. The thick feet offer tons of warmth, and the unique cable construction in the cuff makes them fascinating to stitch. They definitely will survive a lot of wear and tear.

❋ **DESIGNED BY KIM KOTARY** ❋

STITCH GUIDE

Fsc (Foundation single crochet)
Start with a slipknot, ch 2, insert hook in 2nd ch from hook, yarn over and draw up a loop, yarn over and draw through 1 loop (the chain), yarn over and draw through 2 loops (the sc). The following stitch is worked under the forward 2 loops of the stem of the previous stitch (into the chain). *Insert hook into the face of the chain and under the nub at the back of the chain, yarn over and draw up a loop, yarn over and draw through 1 loop (the chain), yarn over and draw through 2 loops (the sc). Repeat from * for the length of foundation.

FPtr (Front Post treble crochet)
Yarn over 2 times, insert hook from front to back to front around the post of the corresponding stitch below, yarn over and pull up loop [yarn over, draw through 2 loops on hook] 3 times.

FPdc (Front Post double crochet)
Yarn over, insert hook from front to back to front around post of corresponding stitch below, yarn over and pull up loop [yarn over, draw through 2 loops on hook] 2 times.

BPdc (Back Post double crochet)
Yarn over, insert hook from back to front to back around post of corresponding stitch below, yarn over and pull up loop [yarn over, draw through 2 loops on hook] 2 times.

Sc2tog (Single crochet 2 together)
Insert hook in next stitch, yarn over and pull up loop (2 loops on hook), insert hook in next stitch, yarn over and pull up loop (3 loops on hook), yarn over and draw through all 3 loops on hook.

NOTES

❀ Socks are worked toe up with an afterthought heel.

❀ Foot and heel are worked in continuous rounds without joining.

❀ Cuff and ribbing are worked in joined rounds.

Instructions

Toe

Rnd 1: Ch 2, 17 Fsc. Sc in same ch as last Fsc, place marker, sc in same place as prev st, sc in base of next 16 Fsc, sc in same st as prev st, place marker—36 sts.

Rnd 2 (Inc): *2 sc in next sc, sc in each sc across to one st before next marker, 2 sc in next sc, slip marker; repeat from * once more—40 sts.

Repeat Rnd 2, increasing 4 sts per rnd (before and after markers) until there are 80 sts.

Foot

Remove 1st marker, leaving 2nd marker to indicate end of rnd. Move marker up at end of each rnd as work progresses.

Work even in sc on 80 sts until work measures 8½" (21.5 cm) from beg. Do not fasten off.

Heel Opening

Fold toe flat. Work sc to next fold and place marker. Work 44 Fsc, skip 40 sc, sc in next 40 sc—84 sts.

Next Rnd: Sc in each Fsc and each sc around—84 sc.

Work in continuous rnds on 84 sts for 6 rnds, sl st in next st.

Cuff

Rnds 1 and 2: Ch 3 (counts as dc, here and throughout), dc in each st around —84 dc. Join with sl st in top of beg ch-3. Do not turn.

Rnd 3: Ch 3, dc in next 2 sts, [ch 5, sc around post of dc 2 rows below and 5 sts over, turn, ch 1, 5 sc in ch-sp, turn, dc in next 5 dc, ch 5, sc around post of dc 2 rows below and 5 sts back (so there are 4 sts between the scs 2 rows below), turn, ch 1, 5 sc in ch-sp, dc in next 9 dc] 6 times ending last rep with dc in next 6 dc. Join with sl st in top of beg ch-3. Do not turn.

Rnd 4: Ch 3, dc in next 10 dc, ch 5, sc around post of dc 2 rows below and 1 st over, sc around post of next dc in same row below, ch 5, skip 2 dc, [dc in next 11 dc, ch 5, sc around post of dc 2 rows below and 1 st over, sc around post of next dc in same row below, ch 5, skip 2 dc] 5 times. Join with sl st in top of beg ch-3. Do not turn.

Rnd 5: Ch 3, dc in next dc, [ch 5, sl st in ch on Rnd 3, sl st in sc, ch 1, turn, 5 sc in ch-sp, dc in next 7 dc] 12 times, ending last rep with dc in next 5 dc. Join with sl st in top of beg ch-3. Do not turn.

Rnd 6: Ch 3, dc in next 10 dc, FPtr around dc under the chain 2 rows below, dc in next dc, ch 5, sc around dc 2 rows below and sc around post of next dc in same row below, ch 5, dc in next dc, FPtr around dc under the chain 2 rows below, [dc in next 11 dc, FPtr around dc under the chain 2 rows below, dc in next dc, ch 5, sc around dc 2 rows below and sc around post of next dc in same row below, ch 5, dc in next dc, FPtr around dc under the chain 2 rows below] 5 times. Join with sl st in top of beg ch-3.

Rnd 7: Ch 3, dc in next 2 sts, [*ch 5, (sl st in ch, sl st in sc) of ch below, turn, ch 1, 5 sc in ch-sp*, dc in next 5 sts; rep bet *s once, dc in next 9 sts] 6 times, ending last rep with dc in next 6 sts. Join with sl st in top of beg ch-3.

Rnd 8: Ch 3, dc in next 11 sts, *yo 2 times, insert hook under post st 2 rows below, draw up loop, yo, draw through 2 loops, yo, insert hook in both ch-5 sps, draw up loop, yo, draw through 2 loops, yo, insert hook under post st, draw up loop, yo, draw through 2 loops, yo, draw through 3 loops, [yo, draw through 2 loops] 2 times, skip 2 sts, dc in next 11 sts; rep from *4 more times, ending last rep with dc in next st. Join with sl st in top of beg ch-3.

Rnd 9: Ch 3, dc in next 2 dc, [ch 5, skip 1st ch-sp 2 rows below, sl st in next ch-sp, sl st in sc, turn, ch 1, 5 sc in ch-sp, dc in next 5 sts, ch 5, sl st in skipped ch-sp, sl st in sc, turn, ch 1, 5 sc in ch-sp, dc in next 9 sts] 6 times, ending last rep with dc in next 6 sts. Join with sl st in top of beg ch-3.

Rnd 10: Ch 3, dc in next 11 sts, [ch 5, sc around skipped st 2 rows below, ch 5, dc in next 134 sts] 6 times, ending last rep with dc in next st. Join with sl st to top of beg ch-3.

Rep Rnds 5–10 for desired cuff length. Do not fasten off.

Cuff Ribbing

Rnd 1: Ch 3, dc in each st around—72 st. Join with sl st to top of beg ch-3. Do not turn.

Rnd 2: Ch 2, [FPdc, BPdc] around to last st, FPdc. Join with sl st in top of beg ch-2.

Rep Rnd 2 until ribbing measures 1" (2.5 cm) or desired length. Fasten off.

Heel

Rnd 1: Attach yarn at base of first Fsc in heel opening. Sc in each of 40 skipped sc, sc2tog in base of next 2 Fsc, pm, sc in base of next 40 fsc, sc2tog in base of next 2 fsc, pm—82 sc with 40 sts between markers on each side.

Rnd 2: *Sc in each sc across to 2 sts before next marker, sc2tog, sc in marked sc, sc2tog; repeat from *.

Rep Rnd 2 until there are only 34 sc remaining. Fasten off leaving a long tail for sewing.

Finishing

Turn sock inside out and whipstitch heel opening closed. Weave in ends.

Finished Measurements
36½" (92.5 cm) wide by 12" (30.5 cm) long.

Yarn
Worsted weight (#4 Medium).

Shown here: Blue Sky Alpacas *Alpaca Silk* (50% alpaca, 50% silk; 146 yd [133 m]/50 g): #139 Peacock (1), #126 Brick (2), #128 Plum (3), #147 Crab Apple (4), #145 Guava (5), #138 Garnet (6), #129 Amethyst (7), #132 Ginger (8), #148 Peridot (9), #114 Wisteria (10), #131 Kiwi (11), #137 Sapphire (12), 1 hank each.

Hook
Size E (3.5 mm) or size needed to obtain gauge.

Gauge
One Hexagon motif = 2¼" (5 cm) diameter.

Take time to check gauge.

Light-as-Air Neckerchief

Delicate motifs stitched in fingering-weight yarn make this piece a true masterpiece. It's light as a feather and drapes like a dream—purely luscious. Worn around the neck or as a head kerchief, this is one piece you'll treasure for years to come.

❈ **DESIGNED BY MARYSE ROUDIER** ❈

STITCH GUIDE

Hexagon Motif Pattern

Make an adjustable ring with color A.

Rnd 1 (RS): 12 sc in ring, pull end to close. Join with sl st in first sc. Do not turn.

Rnd 2: Ch 3, dc in next sc, ch 2, [dc in next 2 sc, ch 2) 5 times. Join with sl st in top of beg ch-3. Do not turn. Fasten off color A.

Rnd 3: Join color B in any ch-2 sp. Ch 3, 2 dc, ch 3, 3 dc in same ch-2 sp, ch 1, *(3 dc, ch 3, 3 dc) in next ch-2 sp, ch 1; rep from * 4 more times. Join with sl st in top of beg ch-3. Fasten off.

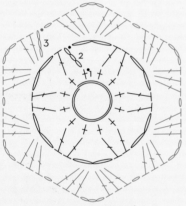

Hexagon Motif

Stitch Key

⬭	chain (ch)
•	slip st (sl st)
+	single crochet (sc)
†	double crochet (dc)
◯	adjustable ring

Instructions

Note: Follow diagram beg at left edge for color combinations, placement, and joining of motifs.

Stripe 1 *(16 motifs)*

FIRST MOTIF

Work Rnds 1–3 of patt for first motif.

SECOND MOTIF

Work Rnds 1 and 2 of patt.

Rnd 3 (Joining): Join color B in any ch-2 sp. Ch 3, (2 dc, ch 3, 3 dc) in same ch-2 sp, ch 1, (3 dc, ch 1, sl st in ch-3 sp of prev motif, ch 1, 3 dc) in next ch-2 sp, sl st in ch-1 sp of prev motif, (3 dc, ch 1, sl st in ch-2 sp of prev motif, ch 1, 3 dc) in next ch-2 sp, ch 1, *(3 dc, ch 3, 3 dc) in next ch-2 sp, ch 1; rep from * twice more. Join with sl st in top of beg ch-3. Fasten off.

THIRD TO SIXTEENTH MOTIFS

Rep as for 2nd motif joining in Rnd 3 to complete Stripe 1. Lay aside with RS facing up.

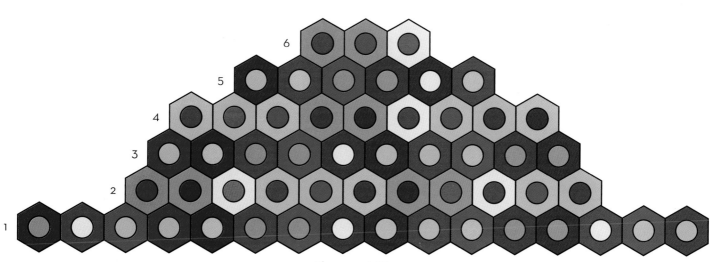

Placement Diagram

Color Chart

■	Peacock (1)	■	Amethyst (7)
■	Brick (2)	■	Ginger (8)
■	Plum (3)	■	Peridot (9)
■	Crab Apple (4)	■	Wisteria (10)
■	Guava (5)	■	Kiwi (11)
■	Garnet (6)	■	Sapphire (12)

Stripe 2 *(11 motifs)*

FIRST MOTIF

Work Rnds 1 and 2 of patt. Join to 3rd and 4th motifs of Stripe 1 as folls:

Rnd 3 (Joining): Join color B in any ch-2 sp. Ch 3, (2 dc, ch 3, 3 dc) in same ch-2 sp, ch 1, (3 dc, ch 3, 3 dc) in next ch-2 sp, ch 1, (3 dc, ch 1, sl st in ch-3 sp of 3rd motif of Stripe 1, ch 1, 3 dc) in next ch-2 sp, sl st in ch-1 sp of 3rd motif of Stripe 1, (3 dc, ch 1, sl st tog ch-3 sp of 3rd and 4th motifs of Stripe 1, ch 1, 3 dc) in next ch-2 sp, sl st in ch-1 sp of 4th motif

of Stripe 1, (3 dc, ch 1, sl st in ch-3 sp of 4th motif of Stripe 1, ch 1, 3 dc) in next ch-2 sp, ch 1, (3 dc, ch 3, 3 dc) in next ch-2 sp, ch 1. Join with sl st in top of beg ch-3. Fasten off.

SECOND MOTIF

Work Rnds 1 and 2 of patt.

Rnd 3 (Joining): Join color B in any ch-2 sp. Ch 3, (2 dc, ch 3, 3 dc) in same ch-2 sp, ch 1, (3 dc, ch 1, sl st in ch-3 sp of prev motif, ch 1, 3 dc) in next ch-2 sp, sl st in ch-1 sp of prev motif, (3 dc, ch 1, sl st tog ch-3 sp of prev motif and 4th motif of Stripe 1, ch 1, 3 dc) in next ch-2 sp, sl st in ch-1 sp of 4th motif of Stripe 1, (3 dc, ch 1, sl st tog ch-3 sp of 4th and 5th motifs of Stripe 1, ch 1, 3 dc) in next ch-2 sp, sl st in ch-1 sp of 5th motif of Stripe 1, (3 dc, ch 1, sl st in ch-3 sp of 5th motif of Stripe 1, ch 1, 3 dc) in next ch-2 sp, ch 1, (3 dc, ch 3, 3 dc) in next ch-2 sp, ch 1. Join with sl st in top of beg ch-3. Fasten off.

THIRD TO ELEVENTH MOTIFS

Rep as for 2nd motif joining in Rnd 3 to complete Stripe 2 and joining to Stripe 1. Lay aside with RS facing up.

Stripes 3 to 6

Rep as for Stripe 2 foll diagram.

Edging

With RS facing, attach color 2 (brick) in any dc st.

Rnd 1 (RS): Ch 1, sc same dc, *work sc in each dc and ch-1 sps, 3 sc in ch-3 sps, work sc in each ch-3 sp where motifs are joined; rep from * around. Join with sl st in first sc. Do not turn. Fasten off. Attach color 5 (guava).

Rnd 2: Ch 1, sc in same sc and in each sc around. Join with sl st in first sc. Fasten off.

Finishing

Weave in ends. Block to measurements.

Stitch Key

⬯ chain (ch)

• slip st (sl st)

✝ single crochet (sc)

† double crochet (dc)

◯ adjustable ring

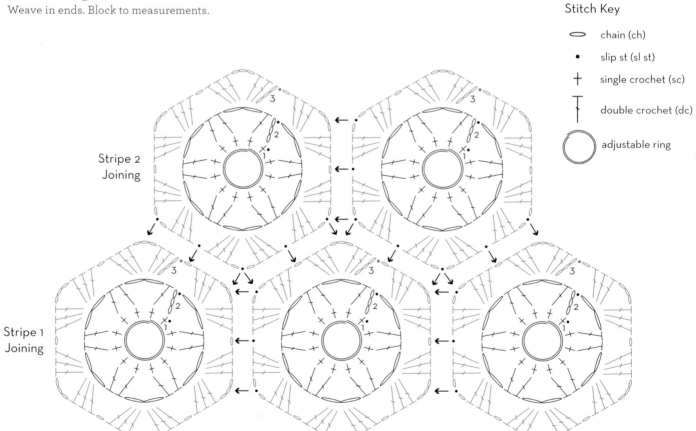

Stripe 2 Joining

Stripe 1 Joining

Finished Measurements

58" (147.5 cm) wide by 34" (86.5 cm) long.

Circumference: about 8" (20.5 cm).

Yarn

Sport/Baby weight (#2 Fine).

Shown here: Filatura di Crosa *Zarina,* (100% extrafine merino wool; 180 yd [165 m]/1.75 oz [50 g]): #1468 Charcoal Gray, 6 balls.

Hook

Size E (3.5 mm) or size needed to obtain gauge.

Gauge

One block rep = 3" (7.5 cm) wide and 2" (5 cm) long.

Take time to check gauge.

Geometry Shawl

An angular lace pattern stitched in lightweight yarn makes this shawl gorgeously drapey and lush to the touch. Wrap it around the neck as a scarf or wear it over the shoulders as a traditional shawl—the long back adds a hint of drama.

❊ DESIGNED BY MARI LYNN PATRICK ❊

Instructions

Beg at the top edge, ch 372. Work in Alternating Twined Block Pattern as foll:

Row 1: Dc in 4th ch from hook, dc in each of next 8 ch, *ch 10, skip 10 ch, dc in each of next 10 ch; rep from * to end. Turn.

Row 2: Ch 3 (counts as dc), dc in next dc, *[ch 2, skip 2 dc, dc in each of next 2 dc] twice, ch 5, sc in next ch-10 sp, ch 5, dc in each of next 2 dc; rep from *, end ch 2, skip 2 dc, dc in each of next 2 dc, ch 2, skip 2 dc, dc in next dc, dc in top of t-ch—19 block pats. Turn.

Row 3: Ch 3 (counts as dc), dc in next dc, *2 dc in next ch-2 sp, ch 2, skip 2 dc, 2 dc in next ch-2 sp, dc in each of next 2 dc, ch 5, sc in next sc, ch 5, dc in each of next 2 dc; rep from *, end 2 dc in next ch-2 sp, ch 2, 2 dc in next ch-2 sp, dc in next dc, dc in top of t-ch. Turn.

Row 4: Ch 3 (counts as dc), dc in next dc, *[ch 2, skip 2 dc, dc in each of next 2 dc] twice, ch 5, sc in next sc, ch 5, dc in each of next 2 dc; rep from *, end ch 2, skip 2 dc, dc in each of next 2 dc, ch 2, skip 2 dc, dc in next dc, dc in top of t-ch. Turn.

Row 5: Ch 3 (counts as dc), dc in next dc, *[2 dc in ch-2 sp, dc in each of next 2 dc] twice, ch 10, dc in each of next 2 dc; rep from *, end [2 dc in ch-2 sp, dc in each of next 2 dc] twice. Turn.

Row 6: (Dec) Ch 5, skip first and next 4 dc, sc in next dc, ch 6, [10 dc in ch-10 sp, ch 10] 17 times, 10 dc in ch-10 sp, ch 6, skip 4 dc, sc in next dc. Turn.

Row 7: Ch 4, dc in ch-6 sp, ch 3, *[dc in each of next 2 dc, ch 2, skip 2 dc] twice, dc in each of next 2 dc, ch 5, sc in ch-10 sp, ch 5; rep from *, end [dc in each of next 2 dc, ch 2, skip 2 dc] twice, dc in each of next 2 dc, then ch 3, dc in ch-6 sp, ch 4, sc in next sc. Turn.

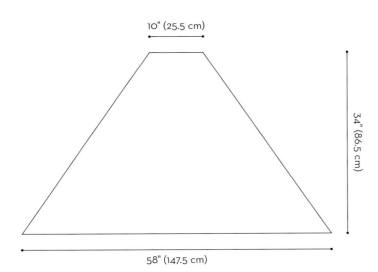

10" (25.5 cm)

34" (86.5 cm)

58" (147.5 cm)

Row 8: Ch 6, sc in next dc, *ch 5, dc in each of next 2 dc, 2 dc in ch-2 sp, ch 2, 2 dc in next ch-2 sp, dc in each of next 2 dc, ch 5, sc in next sc; rep from *, end last rep with ch 6, sc in next dc. Turn.

Row 9: Ch 1, sl st in sc and in each of next 5 ch, ch 3, *[dc in each of next 2 dc, ch 2, skip 2 dc] twice, dc in each of next 2 dc, ch 5, sc in sc, ch 5; rep from *, end with [dc in each of 2 dc, ch 2, skip 2 dc] twice, dc in each of next 2 dc—18 block patts. Turn.

Row 10: Rep Row 5.

Rep Rows 6–10, diminishing by one block patt on each consecutive rep until there are 3 rem complete block patts. Do not fasten off. Turn.

Outer Edge Trim

Next Rnd (RS): [Ch 6, sc in next st] 4 times in each complete block patt and 4 times in each block patt rep along the side rows. Join with sl st in first ch of beg ch-6. Turn.

Rnd 2: [*Ch 4, sc in ch-6 sp; rep from * along side edge to top (beg chain) edge, **ch 5, 1 sc in ch-6 sp; rep from ** across top (beg chain) edge]. Rep bet [ ]s once more, working along opposite side and across bottom edge (lower 3 blocks). Join with sl st in first ch of beg ch-4. Turn.

Rnd 3: Ch 3, 4 dc in 1st ch-5 sp, sl st in next ch-sp, [*5 dc in next ch-sp, sl st in next ch-sp; rep from * across the bottom edge (lower 3 blocks) to side edge, **(sc, 2 hdc, 2 dc) in ch-4 sp, sl st in next ch-sp; rep from ** along one side edge]. Rep bet [ ]s once more working across top edge and opposite side. Join with sl st to top of beg ch-3. Fasten off.

Finishing

Weave in ends. Block to measurements.

Finished Measurements

20½" (52 cm) circumference, unstretched.

Note: Hat will stretch to fit 20–23" (51–58.5 cm) circumference.

Yarn

Worsted weight (#4 Medium).

Shown here: Berroco *Ultra Alpaca* (50% alpaca, 50% wool; 215 yd [198 m]/3.5 oz [100 g]): #6206 Light Gray (MC) and #6289 Charcoal Mix (CC), 1 hank each.

Hook

Size H/8 (5 mm) or size needed to obtain gauge.

Notions

Tapestry needle; stitch marker (optional).

Gauge

14 sts and 14 rnds = 4" (10 cm) in wave pattern using H/8 (5 mm) hook.

Take time to check gauge.

Sedimentary Hat

Stitches of varying heights create a wave-like effect in this cap, for an effect that's reminiscent of the earth's layers. The result is a look that's understated enough to appeal to most men's taste, yet still interesting to stitch. It's the perfect understated gift for yourself or a special man in your life.

❋ DESIGNED BY KJ HAY ❋

Back Loop Only (blo)

STITCH GUIDE

Fhdc (Foundation half-double crochet)
Ch 3, yarn over, insert hook in 3rd chain from hook, yarn over and pull up loop (3 loops on hook), yarn over and draw through 1 loop (1 chain made), yarn over and draw through all loops on hook—1 foundation half double crochet. *Yarn over, insert hook under the 2 loops of the chain stitch of last stitch and pull up loop, yarn over and draw through 1 loop, yarn over and draw through all loops on hook; repeat from * for length of foundation.

Esc (Extended single crochet)
Insert hook in indicated st and draw up a loop, yarn over and draw through first loop on hook, yarn over and draw through both loops on hook.

FPtr (Front Post treble crochet)
[Yarn over] twice, insert hook from front to back then to front again, around post of indicated st and draw up a loop to current working height, [yarn over and draw through 2 loops on hook] 3 times.

Slst2tog (Slip stitch 2 together)
Insert hook in next st and draw up a loop, insert hook in next st and draw loop through st and through loop on hook.

NOTE

❀ To change color, work last st of old color to last yarn over. Yarn over with new color and draw through all loops on hook to complete st. Proceed with new color. Do not fasten off old color. Carry color not in use up inside of hat until next needed.

Instructions

Ribbing

With MC, Fhdc 72; sl st in first Fhdc to form ring.

Rnd 1: (RS)—Ch 2 (does not count as st), *FPtr around next st, dc in next st; rep from * around, sl st in top of beg ch to join—36 FPtr and 36 dc. Do not turn.

Rnd 2: Ch 2, *dc in next st, FPtr around next st; rep from * around, sl st in top of beg ch to join. Do not turn.

Rnd 3: Ch 1, sc in each st around, do not join. Do not turn.

Crown

Note: Crown is worked in continuous rnds; do not join at end of rnds.

You may wish to place a marker for beg of rnd and move marker up as work progresses.

Rnd 4: *Sl st in next st, sc in next 2 sts, esc in next 2 sts, dc in next 2 sts, esc in next 2 sts, sc in next 2 sts, sl st in next st; rep from * around. Change to CC.

Rnd 5: With CC, sl st blo in each st around. Change to MC.

Rnd 6: With MC and working in blo of all sts, ch 2 (does not count as a st) *dc in next st, esc in next 2 sts, sc in next 2 sts, sl st in next 2 sts, sc in next 2 sts, esc in next 2 sts, dc in next st; rep from * around. Change to CC.

Rnd 7: Rep Rnd 5.

Rnd 8: With MC and working in blo of all sts, *sl st in next st, sc in next st, esc in next st, dc in next st, esc in next st, sc in next st; repeat from * around. Change to CC.

Rnd 9: Rep Rnd 5.

Rnd 10: With MC and working in blo of all sts, *dc in next st, esc in next st, sc in next st, sl st in next st, sc in next st, esc in next st; rep from * around. Change to CC.

Rnd 11: Rep Rnd 5.

Rnd 12: With MC and working in blo of all sts, rep Rnd 4.

Rnds 13–19: Rep Rnds 5–11.

Rnd 20: With MC and working in blo of all sts, *sl st in next st, sc in next st, esc in next st, dc in next 2 sts, esc in next st, sc in next st, sl st in next st; rep from * around. Change to CC.

Rnd 21: Rep Rnd 5.

Rnd 22: With MC and working in blo of all sts, ch 2, *dc in next st, esc in next st, sc in next st, sl st in next 2 sts, sc in next st, esc in next st, dc in next st; rep from * around. Change to CC.

Rnd 23: Rep Rnd 5.

Rnd 24: Rep Rnd 20.

SHAPE CROWN

Rnd 25: With CC, [sl st blo in next 6 sts, slst2tog blo] 8 times—56 sts. Change to MC.

Rnd 26: Rep Rnd 20.

Rnd 27: With CC, [sl st blo in next 5 sts, slst2tog blo] 8 times—48 sts. Change to MC.

Rnd 28: Rep Rnd 20.

Rnd 29: With CC, [sl st blo in next 4 sts, slst2tog blo] 8 times—40 sts. Change to MC.

Rnd 30: Rep Rnd 20.

Rnd 31: With CC, [sl st blo in next 3 sts, slst2tog blo] 8 times—32 sts. Change to MC.

Rnd 32: Rep Rnd 20.

Rnd 33: With CC, [sl st blo in next 2 sts, slst2tog blo] 8 times—24 sts. Change to MC.

Rnd 34: Rep Rnd 20. Fasten off MC.

Rnd 35: With CC, [sl st blo in next st, slst2tog blo] 8 times—16 sts. Fasten off CC, leaving a long tail. Weave tail through sts of last rnd and pull to gather and close opening. Weave in tail securely.

Finishing

Weave in all ends.

Size
To fit Average (Plus) size.

Finished Measurements
Length from back neck, including collar: 23" (58.5 cm).

Width at collar (foundation edge): 27 (31)" [68.5 (78.5) cm)]

Width at lower edge: 80 (88)" [203 (223.5) cm)]

Yarn
Heavy worsted weight (#4 Medium).

Shown here: Blue Sky Alpacas *Techno*, (68% baby alpaca, 10% extrafine merino wool, 22% silk; 120 yd [109 m]/1.75 oz [50 g]): #1976 Cha-Cha Red, 5 (7) hanks.

Hook
Size J/10 (6 mm) or size needed to obtain gauge.

Notions
Size 50 (25 mm) Broomstick knitting needle (stick), 1" (2.5 cm) diameter by 14" (35.5 cm) long; stitch markers; tapestry needle.

Gauge
13 sts = 4" (10 cm); 2 patt st rep and 2 patt row rep = 3" (7.5 cm) by 5½" (14 cm) in Broomstick lace patt using size 50 (25 mm) needle.

Take time to check gauge.

Chunky Capelet

Broomstick lace and a heavy yarn make this capelet lightning fast to stitch and beautiful to wear. Available in two sizes that have plenty of comfort and swing, it's perfect over jeans on a crisp fall day. Fasten it with your favorite shawl pin.

❀ **DESIGNED BY DORIS CHAN** ❀

Fsc (Foundation single crochet)

Start with a slipknot, ch 2, insert hook in 2nd ch from hook, yarn over and draw up a loop, yarn over and draw through 1 loop (the chain), yarn over and draw through 2 loops (the sc). The following stitch is worked under the forward 2 loops of the stem of the previous stitch (into the chain). *Insert hook into the face of the chain and under the nub at the back of the chain, yarn over and draw up a loop, yarn over and draw through 1 loop (the chain), yarn over and draw through 2 loops (the sc). Repeat from * for the length of foundation.

Sh (Shell)

3 dc in same sc as indicated.

Broomstick Technique and Tips

Broomstick lace is made with the use of a large-gauge knitting needle (stick) to hold all the loops in a row. Then, using a crochet hook, the loops are held together in groups and worked off the stick with regular crochet stitches. This pattern uses groups of 5 loops, with 5 sc in each group.

For this particular method of Broomstick technique, the stick is held to the left (for right-handed crocheters), and the two steps of this technique are made with RS facing. In the first step, you may need to snug up each loop after slipping it to the stick to keep all the loops as even as possible. Do not tighten the loops too much as the row of loops on the stick should slide freely to be easily worked off in the second step.

Note: To slip a loop from the crochet hook onto the stick, keep the loop seated in the same direction (in knitting terms that means slip as if to purl). Bring the hook to the tip of the stick, slip the loop across without twisting, so the strand that lies to the front of the hook ends up at the front of the stick.

Loop Row (RS): At the end of a regular crochet row, do not turn. Slip the last loop on hook onto the stick (counts as first loop). Moving from left to right (backward across the row of regular crochet), skip first sc, *insert empty hook through back loop only of next sc, yarn over and draw up a loop long enough to fit over the stick. Slip the loop onto the stick as described above, without twisting; repeat from * across the row as directed, do not turn.

Return Row (RS): Insert empty hook from right to left in the first 5 loops on stick, keeping loops seated in same direction. Holding the 5 loops in a group and working the group as one, slide the group off the stick. Pick up the feeder yarn from the back of the row, bring yarn loosely up to the level of the hook, yarn over and draw a loop through the group, ch 1 to lock the edge (1 loop on hook). This is the only place you will need to ch 1 before making a stitch. Working the group as one, make 5 sc in the same group. *Insert hook in next 5 loops on stick, slide group off the stick, 5 sc in group; repeat from *across, turn.

❈ Capelet is roughly a half-circle, crocheted from the collar edge down, with increase shaping in stitch pattern to form the shoulders and flare the body.

❈ All increase shaping is done in the rows of regular crochet stitches. All Broomstick loop rows and return rows are straightforward and even.

❈ To alter the length of the capelet, you may omit or add repeats of the 8-row stitch pattern (Rows 11–18, alternating increase ch-sp rows with even ch-sp rows) as established.

Instructions

85 (95) Fsc. Turn foundation over so sc edge is on top and to begin work across sc edge.

Row 1 (loop row) (RS): Following broomstick loop row instructions above, pull up a loop for each sc across—85 (95) loops on stick. Do not turn.

Row 2 (return row) (RS): Following return row instructions above, work 5 sc in each group of 5 loops—85 (95) sc in 17 (19) groups of 5. Turn.

Row 3 (ch-sp row) (WS): Ch 5 (counts as dc and ch 2), skip first 2 sc, sc in next sc (at center of group), *ch 5, skip next 4 sc, sc in next sc (at center of

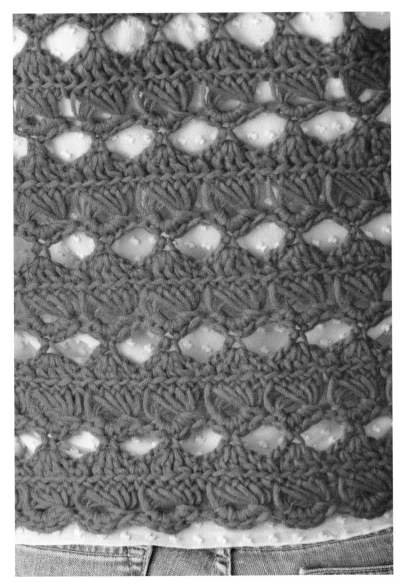

Row 5 (loop row): Work Broomstick loop row—85 (95) loops on stick. Do not turn.

Row 6 (return row): Work 5 sc in each group of 5 loops—85 (95) sc in 17 (19) groups of 5. Turn.

Size Average Only

Row 7 (Inc ch-sp row): Ch 5 (counts as dc and ch 2), skip first 2 sc, sc in next sc (at center of group), [ch 5, skip next 4 sc, sc in next sc (at center of group)] 3 times, *[skip next 4 sc, (ch 5, sc) 2 times in next sc for increase] 4 times*, ch 5, skip next 4 sc, sc in next sc (at center back neck); rep from * to * once, [ch 5, skip next 4 sc, sc in next sc] 4 times, end with ch 2, skip next sc, dc in last sc—24 ch-5 sps plus edge sps, 25 sc. Turn.

Mark the 6th, 10th, 16th, and 20th sc, move markers up as you go into the center at each location.

Size Plus Only

Row 7 (Inc ch-sp row): Ch 5 (counts as dc and ch 2), skip first 2 sc, sc in next sc (at center of group), [ch 5, skip next 4 sc, sc in next sc (at center of group)] 3 times, [skip next 4 sc, (ch 5, sc) 2 times in next sc for increase] 11 times, [ch 5, skip next 4 sc, sc in next sc] 4 times, end with ch 2, skip next sc, dc in last sc—29 ch-5 sps plus edge sps, 30 sc. Turn.

Mark the 7th, 12th, 19th, and 24th sc, move or wrap markers up as you go into the center at each location.

All Sizes

Rows 8–10: Repeat Rows 4–6—125 (150) sc in 25 (30) groups of 5. Turn.

There are markers in the center sc of the 6th, 10th, 16th, and 20th (7th, 12th, 19th, and 24th) groups of 5.

Make increase ch-sps in the groups before and after each marked group as folls:

group); rep from * across to last 2 sc, ch 2, skip next sc, dc in last sc—16 (18) ch-5 sps plus edge sps. Turn.

Row 4 (shell row) (RS): Ch 1, sc in first dc, *Sh in next sc, skip next 2 ch, 2 sc in next ch (at center of ch-5 sp); rep from * across to last sc, Sh in last sc, sc in 3rd ch of t-ch—17 (19) shells, 85 (95) sts. Do not turn.

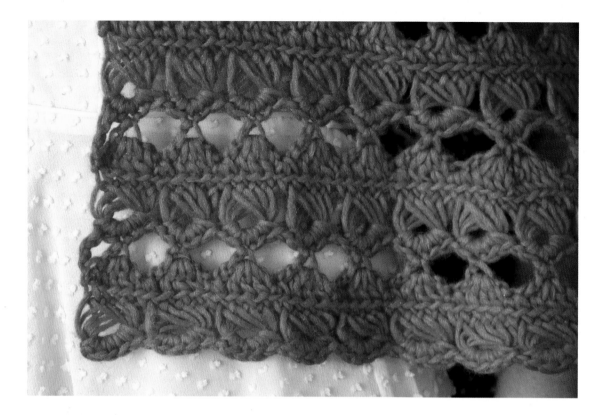

Row 11 (Inc ch-sp row): Ch 5 (counts as dc and ch 2), skip first 2 sc, sc in next sc (at center of group), *[ch 5, skip next 4 sc, sc in next sc (at center of group)] to the group *before* next marker, skip next 4 sc, [ch 5, sc] 2 times in next sc for increase, ch 5, skip next 4 sc, sc in next sc at marker, skip next 4 sc, [ch 5, sc] 2 times in next sc *after* marker for increase*; rep from * 3 times more, [ch 5, skip next 4 sc, sc in next sc (at center of group)] across, end with ch 2, skip next sc, dc in last sc—32 (37) ch-5 sps plus edge sps, 33 (38) sc. Turn.

Rows 12–14: Repeat Rows 4–6—165 (190) sc in 33 (38) groups of 5.

Row 15 (ch-sp row): Repeat Row 3.

Rows 16–18: Repeat Rows 4–6.

Row 19 (Inc ch-sp row): Repeat Rows 11–40 (45) ch-5 sps plus edge sps, 41 (46) sc.

Rows 20–26: Repeat Rows 12–18—205 (230) sc in 41 (46) groups of 5.

Row 27 (Inc ch-sp row): Repeat Rows 11–48 (53) ch-5 sps plus edge sps, 49 (54) sc.

Rows 28–34: Repeat Rows 12–18—245 (270) sc in 49 (54) groups of 5. Fasten off.

Finishing

Weave in ends.

Block capelet by dampening capelet with cool water, then spread out flat in a half-circle. It will be necessary to fold back the collar to make the neckline lie flat. Ease into shape and to measurements. Allow to dry completely.

Abbreviations

beg	begin; begins; beginning
bet	between
ch(s)	chain(s)
cl(s)	cluster(s)
cm	centimeter(s)
cont	continue(s); continuing
dc	double crochet
dec	decrease(s); decreasing; decreased
dtr	double treble (triple)
est	established
foll	follows; following
g	gram(s)
hdc	half double crochet
inc	increase(s); increasing; increased
lp(s)	loop(s)
MC	main color
m	marker
mm	millimeter(s)
p	picot
patt	pattern(s)
pm	place marker
rem	remain(s); remaining
rep	repeat; repeating
rev sc	reverse single crochet
rnd(s)	round(s)
RS	right side
sc	single crochet
sk	skip

sl	slip
sl st	slip(ped) stitch
sp(s)	space(s)
st(s)	stitch(es)
t-ch	turning chain
tog	together
tr	treble crochet
tr tr	triple treble crochet
TSS	Tunisian simple stitch
WS	wrong side
*	repeat starting point
WS	wrong side
yd	yard(s)
yo	yarn over
()	alternate measurements and/or instructions

Techniques

Ch (chain st)

Make a slipknot and place it on crochet hook. *Yarn over hook and draw through loop on hook. Repeat from * for the desired number of stitches.

Sl st (slip stitch)

*Insert hook into stitch, yarn over hook and draw loop through stitch and loop on hook. Repeat from *.

Sc (single crochet)

Insert hook into a stitch, yarn over hook and draw up a loop (**FIGURE 1**), yarn over hook and draw it through both loops on hook (**FIGURE 2**).

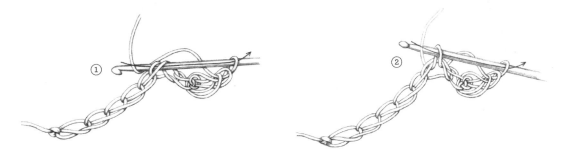

Dc (double crochet)

*Yarn over hook, insert hook into a stitch, yarn over hook and draw up a loop (3 loops on hook; **FIGURE 1**), yarn over hook and draw it through 2 loops (**FIGURE 2**), yarn over hook and draw it through remaining 2 loops on hook (**FIGURE 3**). Repeat from *.

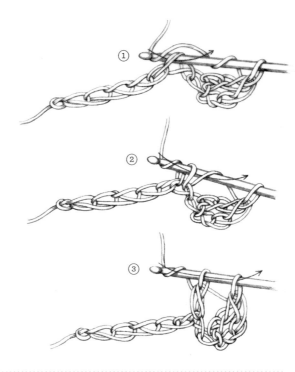

Tr (treble crochet)

*Wrap yarn around hook twice, insert hook into next indicated stitch, yarn over hook and draw up a loop (4 loops on hook; **FIGURE 1**), yarn over hook and draw it through 2 loops (**FIGURE 2**), yarn over hook and draw it through the next 2 loops, yarn over hook and draw it through the remaining 2 loops on hook (**FIGURE 3**). Repeat from *.

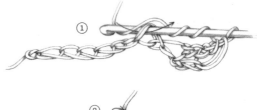

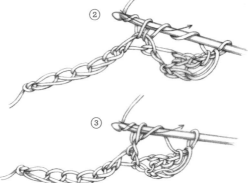

FPdc
(Front Post double crochet)

Yarn over hook, insert hook from front to back to front again around post of stitch indicated, yarn over hook and pull up a loop (3 loops on hook), [yarn over hook and draw through 2 loops on hook] twice—1 fpdc made.

BPdc
(Back Post double crochet)

Yarn over hook, insert hook from back to front, to back again around the post of stitch indicated, yarn over hook, draw yarn through stitch, [yarn over hook, draw yarn through 2 loops on hook] twice.

Sc2tog
(single crochet 2 together)

Insert hook into stitch and draw up a loop. Insert hook into next stitch and draw up a loop. Yarn over hook (FIGURE 1). Draw through all 3 loops on hook (FIGURES 2 AND 3).

Fsc
(foundation single crochet)

Ch 2 (**FIGURE 1**), insert hook in 2nd ch from hook (**FIGURE 2**), yarn over hook and draw up a loop (2 loops on hook), yarn over hook, draw yarn through first loop on hook (**FIGURE 3**), yarn over hook and draw through 2 loops on hook (**FIGURE 4**)—1 fsc made (**FIGURE 5**).

*Insert hook under 2 loops of ch made at base of previous stitch (**FIGURE 6**), yarn over hook and draw up a loop (2 loops on hook), yarn over hook and draw through first loop on hook, yarn over hook and draw through 2 loops on hook (**FIGURE 7**). Repeat from * for length of foundation.

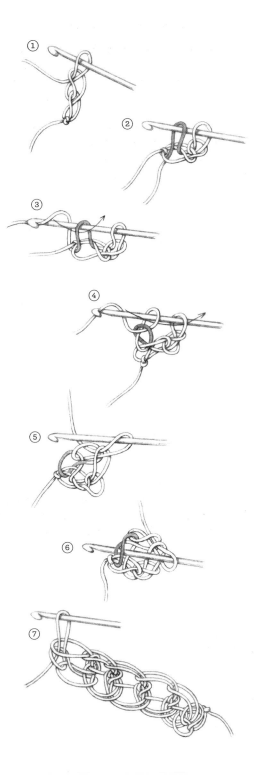

Making an adjustable ring

Make a large loop with the yarn (**FIGURE 1**). Holding the loop with your fingers, insert hook into loop and pull working yarn through loop (**FIGURE 2**). Yarn over hook, pull through loop on hook.

Continue to work indicated number of stitches into loop (**FIGURE 3**; shown in single crochet). Pull on yarn tail to close loop (**FIGURE 4**).

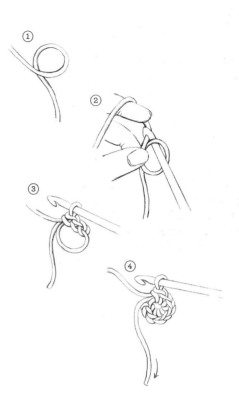

Whipstitch seam

With right sides of work facing and working through edge stitches, bring threaded needle out from back to front, along edge of piece.

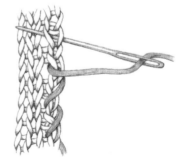

Sources for Yarns

Alchemy Yarns of Transformation
PO Box 1080
Sebastopol, CA 95473
(707) 823-3276
alchemyyarns.com

Berroco Inc.
1 Tupperware Dr., Ste. 4
N. Smithfield, RI 02896
(401) 769-1212
berroco.com

Bijou Basin Ranch
PO Box 154
Elbert, CO 80106
(303) 601-7544
bijoubasinranch.com

Blue Sky Alpacas
(888) 460-8862
blueskyalpacas.com

Caron
320 Livingstone Ave. South
Box 40
Listowel, ON
Canada N4W 3H3
(888) 368-8401
caron.com

Cascade Yarns
cascadeyarns.com

Classic Elite Yarns
16 Esquire Rd., Unit 2
North Billerica, MA 01862
(800) 343-0308
classiceliteyarns.com

Habu Textiles
135 West 29th St.
Ste. 804
New York, NY 10001
(212) 239-3546
habutextiles.com

Knit Picks
(800) 574-1323
knitpicks.com

Rowan Yarns
Green Lane Mill
Holmfirth
West Yorkshire
England HD9 2DX
knitrowan.com
Distributed in the U.S.
by Westminster Fibers

Kollage Yarns
3591 Cahaba Beach Rd.
Birmingham, AL 35242
(888) 829-7758
kollageyarns.com

Madelinetosh
7515 Benbrook Pkwy.
Benbrook, TX 76126
(817) 249-3066
madelinetosh.com

Malabrigo Yarn
(786) 866-6187
malabrigoyarn.com

Noro Yarns
Distributed in the U.S.
by Knitting Fever
noroyarns.com
knittingfever.com

Red Heart
PO Box 12229
Greenville, SC 29612-0229
(800) 648-1479
shopredheart.com

Spud and Chloë
Blue Sky Alpacas
PO Box 88
Cedar, MN 55011
(888) 460-8862
spudandchloe.com

Tahki-Stacy Charles Inc.
70-60 83rd St., Bldg. #12
Glendale, NY 11385
(718) 326-4433
tahkistacycharles.com

The Fibre Company
Distributed By Kelbourne
Woolens
2000 Manor Rd.
Conshohocken, PA 19428
(484) 368-3666
thefibreco.com
kelbournewoolens.com

Universal Yarn
universalyarn.com

Westminster Fibers
165 Ledge St.
Nashua, NH 03060
(800) 445-9276
westminsterfibers.com

Index

get hooked
on these other great Interweave resources

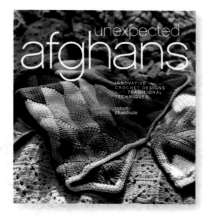

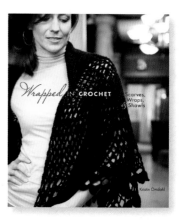

Unexpected Afghans
Innovative Crochet Designs
with Traditional Techniques
Robyn Chachula
ISBN 978-1-59668-299-3
$22.95

Simply Crochet
22 Stylish Designs
for Every Day
Robyn Chachula
ISBN 978-1-59668-298-6
$22.95

Wrapped in Crochet
Scarves, Wraps & Shawls
Kristin Omdahl
ISBN 978-1-59668-076-0
$22.95

crochetme shop
shop.crochetme.com

INTERWEAVE CROCHET

From cover to cover, *Interweave Crochet* magazine presents great projects for the beginner to the advanced crocheter. Every issue is packed full of captivating designs, step-by-step instructions, easy-to-understand illustrations, plus well-written, lively articles sure to inspire. Interweavecrochet.com

crochetme
fueling the crochet revolution

Want to CrochetMe? *Crochet Me* is an online community that shares your passion for all things crochet. Browse through our free patterns, read our blogs, check out our galleries, chat in the forums, make a few friends. Sign up at Crochetme.com.